The Age of Precarity

The Age of Precarity

Endless Crisis as an
Art of Government

Dario Gentili

Translated by
Stefania Porcelli
in collaboration with
Clara Pope

VERSO
London • New York

First published by Verso 2021
© Dario Gentili 2021
Translation © Stefania Porcelli, in collaboration with Clara Pope 2021

1 3 5 7 9 10 8 6 4 2

Verso
UK: 6 Meard Street, London W1F 0EG
US: 20 Jay Street, Suite 1010, Brooklyn, NY 11201
versobooks.com

Verso is the imprint of New Left Books

ISBN-13: 978-1-78873-380-9
ISBN-13: 978-1-78873-793-7 (HB)
ISBN-13: 978-1-78873-382-3 (US EBK)
ISBN-13: 978-1-78873-381-6 (UK EBK)

British Library Cataloguing in Publication Data
A catalogue record for this book is available from the British Library

Library of Congress Cataloging-in-Publication Data
A catalog record for this book is available from the Library of Congress

Typeset in Fournier by MJ & N Gavan, Truro, Cornwall
Printed and bound by CPI Group (UK) Ltd, Croydon, CR0 4YY

Contents

Preface

Ever since 2008, discourses of financial crisis have dominated political language. How are these discourses linked to the way citizens today, across the world, express their opinions on a variety of subjects, through 'likes' or 'dislikes' on social media? Even to venture such a connection might seem hazardous: how can an economic crisis – whose rhetoric pushes states towards making forced decisions – find a counterpart in such a widespread, radically personalized form of criticism? Still, on closer inspection, the choices imposed by the crisis – with their attendant lack of alternatives – have something in common with the reduction of critical practice to a matter of approval or disapproval: they rely on the same mode of judgment 'for or against'.

The judgment for or against – that is, the choice between two opposing alternatives – is today considered to be the mode of judgment par excellence. This is apparent both in matters of public significance and in those concerning individual conduct. It seems to be the model to which every decision-making process must ultimately conform in order to reach a final, conclusive decision about both the life of society and our own personal lives. And yet, although sharply contrasting with one another, the alternatives proposed by the recent crisis are in no way conclusive: they do not put an end to the crisis, nor do they change our own social and existential conditions. It seems, therefore, that although the judgment for or against is today used as frequently and widely as it has ever been, it does not produce any actual decision. This is the most immediate link between the economic crisis and the status of critical practice in the time of social media.

To assess the extent of this connection, let us consider the political use of the for-or-against mode of judgment, which was considered to be a final judgment. First used during the modern period, it assumed its political connotation in times of crisis, when political power was unable to maintain order and had to resort to a definitive decision, which could restore or overthrow the existing order, in either a conservative or a revolutionary direction. To create the conditions for a final, decisive judgment of this kind there must be a state of emergency; it is, in fact, only in crisis that such a judgment becomes 'political', that is, only when the political government in command is no longer able to preserve its power. Is this specifically modern configuration of 'political judgment' still appropriate for describing and understanding the mode of judgment which today characterizes democracies in the West and elsewhere?

More than ever, in today's neoliberal era, the form of judgment for or against dominates not only society and the media, but also the political arena. We need only think of the increasingly frequent recourse to the institution of the referendum, which has tripled since the fall of the Berlin Wall. Referendums all over the world call on people to express their opinions on important political issues. Two recent examples are the 2015 referendum in Greece and the UK's 2016 referendum on Brexit. Despite different referendum questions and different results, in both cases the referendums were seen as the most democratic form of political expression. Is this in fact the case? Or is the referendum simply one of the tools that those who govern – the ruling class – use to legitimize and endorse their own decisions? Doesn't the question on the ballot paper clearly indicate the government's preferred option? We must also be very careful – as in the case of Brexit – not to evaluate a referendum according to its outcome, as if its result could bring about a drastic change of direction in the politics of a country. After all, even when it is not promoted by the government in office but by social and political movements that oppose its policies, the referendum still falls within the remit of the art of government and, whatever its outcome, implies at most a change *within* the logic of government. The real question is what types of politics draw on referendums (and similar instruments) as representing a political judgment par excellence, to such an extent that elections themselves increasingly acquire the meaning of a judgment for or against one or another candidate. Even when a vote is simply for the 'lesser evil' it takes a form equivalent to a 'like' on social media. Similarly, rulings by decree or through votes of confidence, although not directly interrogating the population, also make use of a decision-making mode that, calling upon emergency or exceptional procedures, does not follow the normal process of parliamentary debate and consists essentially in 'approving' of the government in power.

The building of walls, which seemingly belongs to a very different context, is in fact also heavily linked to the judgment for or against in politics. Not only did the recourse to referendums increase after 1989, but, following the fall of the Berlin Wall, 'political walls' throughout the world have multiplied as well. Over thirty border walls already exist, and others are being planned. They represent the need for a judgment for or against, as they define an alternative between two extremes – inside or outside – that is more rigid than ever. Those who are on the wrong side of the wall have only one choice forced upon them: life or death.

The aim of this book is to show that the art of government that draws on these kinds of instruments differs from that which characterized the modern period. Since then, the function of the judgment for or against appears to have profoundly changed, and the context of crisis from which this modality of judgment proceeds is also very different. If, in the modern period, crisis was political – in the sense that politics would intervene to resolve a crisis, whether re-establishing the status quo or overturning it – today we understand it as primarily economic, meaning that financial crises affect and organize political decisions. The very expression 'there is a crisis, there is no alternative', with which governments across the world justify and legitimize unpopular political and economic decisions, cannot be seen simply as a rhetorical strategy. It entails a very specific art of government. Current interpretations of the economic crisis as 'endless' or as 'secular stagnation' date back to at least the 1970s, when neoliberal economic policies started to influence political decisions in some countries. These interpretations fall within the definition of crisis as art of government. Crisis as art of government is the political definition of economic crisis in the neoliberal era.

The neoliberal economic crisis does not produce a 'state of exception' but, to employ an expression used by Walter Benjamin in 1940, has turned 'the exception into the rule'. The neoliberal art of government's contribution to this configuration of crisis consists in the model of political judgment it produces. In fact, even though the form of a judgment for or against remains, its outcome is never a final or conclusive decision as it had been in the modern period, when it could restore or overthrow the existing order to resolve the crisis. The political judgment of neoliberalism is, rather, a judgment that helps *preserve* the order, or, to put it another way, *administers* it. In short, neoliberalism rules by means of the forced decisions brought about by crisis within the given order. The neoliberal crisis therefore establishes a judgment without a final or conclusive decision.

However, although it seems to characterize the neoliberal period and to have appeared with neoliberalism, crisis as art of government has a much longer history, stretching back to the ancient world. To explore this history, I will offer a genealogy of the notion of crisis. We will see that although the neoliberal crisis differs from the idea of crisis in the modern period, it is in line with its pre-modern origin and usage. This genealogical reconstruction therefore inscribes the neoliberal crisis in the long history of the *dispositif* of crisis. Thus, the idea of crisis in the modern era turns out to be no more than a brief parenthesis.

The link between crisis and the judgment for or against has its roots in ancient Greece. Crisis is not simply an opportunity to express one's opinion for or against; the judgment for or against can itself be called crisis. Indeed, the word *krisis* and the corresponding verb *krinein* define a judgment between two different and opposing elements. Yet – and this is its main difference from crisis in modernity – the elements which the judgment of *krisis* has to choose between are not equally viable. Rather, *krisis* is inscribed within a predetermined order, which implies the following: even when facing two extremes, the decision that follows *krisis* is unavoidable and always tends to preserve the existing order that has proclaimed the existence of a crisis. Although this method of judgment was already used by Parmenides, it was with Plato that it found its own place within the political order of the polis. In Plato, the judgment of *krisis* is one of the prerogatives of the rulers and is entrusted to the judges, whose task it is to administer order. However, Plato limited the use of *krisis* to the judicial administration of the city, firmly distinguishing its mode of judgment from the proper political decision – that political decision establishing the order of the polis, organizing and controlling its political life and rule in times of both peace and war. This political decision is the privilege of the assembly. In Plato, just as in Aristotle, the judgment of *krisis* is therefore at the service of the political decision, and the judicial administration of the city is not to be confused with political power; in fact it is submitted to political power.

In ancient Greece, in addition to defining the judicial or forensic judgment, the term *krisis* was used in medicine, first by Hippocrates and later by Galen. In this case too, *krisis* defines a condition in which the judgment is a choice between two extremes: life and death. Crisis corresponds to the time when the sick body is at the peak of its struggle for survival.

Yet, at least for Hippocrates, *krisis* does not involve a real decision on the part of the physician; rather, it defines the moment
in which the body reacts to the disease, and nature's tendency
towards self-preservation prevails. Therefore, even in the case
of ancient medicine, there was no conclusive decision. Rather
than deciding whether the patient lived or died, the physician
was required to diagnose a recovery, which was, however,
already determined by nature itself. Thus death occurs in the
absence of crisis.

Krisis is thus an expression of the natural and bodily self-
preservation of the existing order. Like forensic judgment,
medical judgment also falls within the remit of administration, in this case the administration of the population's health.
Although the physicians' scope is limited to the diagnosis of
the outcome of the disease, their experience means that they
can predict under what conditions a certain disease will occur
and therefore can act to manage the conduct of the population
in order to prevent the spread of the disease, such as in the case
of epidemics. But again, the administration of health is at the
service of political power.

Then as now, 'technicians' – in ancient Greece in the form of
judges and physicians – are in charge of administering the crisis.
The key difference is in the *political* connotation that such 'technical' judgment has today, when the political crisis becomes a
matter of administration and administration becomes the art of
government par excellence.

The term 'crisis' kept this *technical* meaning until the modern
period. In fact, up until the mid-eighteenth century, encyclopaedias and dictionaries of most European languages only reported
the medical meaning of 'crisis'. And it is in analogy with this

medical sense that the word began to enter the economic vocabulary. The medical sense of crisis finally entered political discourse just before the French Revolution. At that point, the judgment for or against – a distinctive trait of Enlightenment critique – emerged as a judgment concerning whether the established political power was healthy or diseased.

Albeit with some caution, Jean-Jacques Rousseau associated the course of medical crisis with the idea of revolution articulated in modernity according to Enlightenment critique, the crisis was no longer meant to preserve the health of the given order; on the contrary, the political body was so sick that only the revolution could regenerate it. The French Revolution provided historical evidence that a political crisis could generate a new order. In this situation, crisis became political and called for a conclusive decision, condemning the previous order to death and establishing a new one.

Karl Marx inherited and radicalized the Enlightenment critique that had become political with the French Revolution. He also tried to introduce this revolutionary sense of crisis and political decision into economic discourse. If, in the *Communist Manifesto*, he considers the economic crisis of capitalism as a way of preserving and reinvigorating the system, in the *Grundrisse* he understands the *dispositif* of economic crisis in a revolutionary sense: crises were symptoms of the capitalist system's fatal disease; only the political revolution and the proletariat that led it could give life to a new order, generating a new life. The crisis of the capitalist economy was no longer instrumental to the self-preservation of the system but tended to overthrow and transform it. Thus, Marx converted the forced decision imposed by the economic crisis into the revolutionary cause.

Antonio Gramsci did not change Marx's diagnosis of the health of the capitalist system but assigned the possibility of exploiting the crisis to the dominant classes rather than to subaltern classes. He defines crisis as the 'interregnum' between the dying old order and a new life which cannot yet be born. The government of this interregnum is primarily a prerogative of the ruling class, and its duration is endless, because crisis itself does not create new life. In fact, crisis is controlled by the ruling class and perfectly performs its function when it gives precedence to the principle of the self-preservation of the current order. Crisis represents a 'mortal danger' and so it forces the subaltern classes to hope for the survival of the current order rather than for its death. Starting with Gramsci, crisis begins to acquire those biopolitical traits that we find in the neoliberal *dispositif* of crisis. It is with neoliberalism that the ruling class becomes the representative of the 'party of life'.

The term 'party of life' was employed by Friedrich von Hayek, one of the key thinkers of neoliberalism, to distinguish his concept of liberalism from previous definitions. In his lecture course on the birth of biopolitics, Michel Foucault used Hayek's term to show that neoliberalism is not simply an alternative technique of government, but an art of government which aims to leave no alternative: the art of neoliberal government crosses class divisions, acting in the name of life. The fact that Hayek supplied a theoretical framework for Margaret Thatcher's biopolitical neoliberal mantra, 'There is no alternative', was not the only reason he played a decisive role in the construction of neoliberal discourse. As early as the 1930s, Hayek began to go beyond the teachings of his mentor Ludwig von Mises, as it became clear that the issue of economic crisis could not be addressed within the theoretical framework of a general economic equilibrium, which considered crisis as an 'unbalance' and aimed to overcome it through the restoration of the economic cycle. Fighting against the Keynesian solution that prevailed after the 1929 crisis, Hayek understood that crises were not a passing and temporary phenomenon and so their function could not be reduced to their solution, that is to re-establishing an equilibrium in the economic cycle. Rather, crises posed the question of 'government'. Hence the market and its cycles were not to be considered according to the criterion of balance, but according to the principle of *order*. Thus Hayek used the expression 'spontaneous order' to define the market. The market governs itself through constant evolution, which individual enterprise helps but does not direct: we might say that the economy is no longer a technical question, but a question of order, and so becomes an art of government. A criticism of the given order and the establishment of a new order is no longer conceivable from outside the status quo. The spontaneous order ensures survival, and subjects left outside of it are doomed. Paraphrasing Thatcher, there is no alternative to adapting to the order.

This brings us back to the idea we explored earlier when looking at ancient Greece, in which *krisis* brought about forced decisions. It is within the spontaneous order of the market that *krisis* can again perform the function it had in the ancient world: the preservation of the order and the legitimation of the rulers' action. To emphasize the discontinuity with the modern political attitude – which turned Enlightenment critique into the criterion of political crisis – Hayek adopts terminology from ancient thought: he uses the word 'catallaxy' to indicate the form of government that emerges from the exchange and market economy, and 'cosmos' to define the spontaneous order of the market. As in Greek tragedy, the cosmos is an order over which human beings have no power. No human being – not even the sovereign – or political revolution can intervene from outside to overturn and overthrow its order. In short, no political power can govern and direct the ends of the spontaneous order of the market as cosmos. The market cosmos governs itself. And it does so by means of crisis, through the administration of power and the administration of the health of bodies. Whereas in Plato crisis was purely administrative, and so at the service of the political order, in neoliberalism it is identical with political power. When political power is reduced to pure management or administration, crisis becomes a form of political judgment.

In its neoliberal configuration, crisis – as art of government – directly rules over the conduct of the individual and the population; this is what allows us to define the current crisis as biopolitical. It is true that the model of judgment of crisis already had the function of controlling individual conduct in ancient Greece, but the use of *krisis* was largely limited to the forensic and medical *techne*. The administration of human conduct gained the traits of biopolitics only when economic discourse – which had been subordinate to politics – became dominant, and when forensic and medical practices began to shape political *techne*. We can see this administration at work today in the Covid-19 pandemic, demonstrating the relentless art of biopolitical government in this crisis, in which medicine, law, and economics are interwoven. Neoliberalism has made this interweaving its art of government.

With neoliberalism, the government of forms of life found its own order in the global market. The discourse of the market controls conduct by means of the constant threat of 'mortal danger', eliciting that sense of vulnerability and precariousness experienced during an epidemic. This includes marginalization, poverty, unemployment – the risk of not surviving if one is not able to compete in the 'meritocracy' of the market. The entrepreneurial risk of the self-employed neoliberal individual always goes hand in hand with the precariousness of their position in the cosmos. This is a condition that entrusts the success or failure of the enterprises to the market, which shares the inscrutability of the cosmos's ends and designs. It is thus no surprise that Hayek writes that human beings – whose form of life is the enterprise – are never the masters of their own destiny. The precariat, then, is the typical figure of labour in the era of neoliberal crisis as art of government. However, it is not limited to those working without a contract or with temporary contracts without guarantees. The precariat is not defined as a class in the socio-economic sense, the form of life of the self-employed entrepreneur is gradually shaping all types of work, even permanent jobs with guarantees and benefits. Crisis as art of government forces decisions from individuals who want to survive in the market, thus affecting their forms of life whatever their employment contract. Precarity is first and foremost the form of life in the age of crisis as art of government.

Although this form of life is only now becoming predominant, it emerged as early as the second half of the nineteenth century, after universal middle-class citizenship had been formalized through the French Revolution and the revolutions that followed – all of which adhered to the modern paradigm of political crisis. On the one hand, the Marxist critique of this outcome led to the call for a proletarian revolution. On the other hand, the uniformity and conformity of universal bourgeois citizenship, along with the undifferentiated masses within the modern metropolises, left unsatisfied the needs of the new subjectivities which had appeared in nineteenth-century Paris. In Walter Benjamin's reconstruction and interpretation, Charles Baudelaire embodied this new type. To stand out from the crowd, and in order to ensure the survival of his own individuality, Baudelaire became an 'entrepreneur of himself', selling his *dandy* form of life on the market. For him the market represented that cosmic order – beyond the order of the state, of citizenship and of the factory – in which he could assert his intellectual and artistic enterprise and emerge as a tragic hero.

At that time, the artist's and the intellectual worker's precariousness allowed them to stand out from the conformity of mass society and the anonymity of the factory. Precarity, however, has become the rule in the post-Fordist era. And the cosmos of the market, which back then could be seen as an alternative to the dominant order of the nation-state and the factory, is now an order that leaves no alternative, overpowering the state itself. Suffice to consider that everywhere in the world technical governments rule over 'states of exception' by enacting reforms that please the market; not to mention the emblematic cases of countries such as Belgium, Spain and the Netherlands, which experienced growth when the economic crisis was at its peak, despite remaining without a political government for long periods of time due to elections that had resulted in a stalemate. Nor do the results of the referendums in Greece and Britain mean a 'return of the state' and of its modern political power, as some have suggested. In both cases, the outcome of the referendum had to conform to the order of the market. The resulting decision was therefore not at all conclusive, but rather part of the model of neoliberal crisis. In other words, this decision would produce more forced decisions in the future. Neither can the so-called 'new populisms' be considered an alternative to neoliberalism, as their stances result from the same precariousness produced by the condition of crisis: their demands for order, security and defence are in line with the government of crisis. An effective alternative to the narrative of the neoliberal cosmos is now necessary. This would be a cosmic narrative that did not present itself to the individual as an inescapable destiny, but as being shared and decided in common, beyond crisis: a new cosmos, in which political decision would be free from judgment by crisis.

I. KRISIS

I'll take another example: that of the constitution of a medico-legal apparatus.

Michel Foucault, 'The Confession of the Flesh'

1

Crisis as *Dispositif*

In the conclusion of his 1982 text on the concept of crisis, Reinhart Koselleck analyses the term 'crisis' etymologically and considers the changes to its meaning in different periods and domains. He implies that the depth of its original Greek meaning gradually faded, with its meaning becoming rather vague during the modern era. Indeed, the wide diffusion of the term might be due to this indeterminacy. Koselleck reaches the following conclusion: 'The concept of crisis, which once had the power to pose unavoidable, harsh and non-negotiable alternatives, has been transformed to fit the uncertainties of whatever might be favored at a given moment.'[1] He argues that there has been a transformation in the purely modern determination of the concept of crisis, 'which once had the power to pose unavoidable, harsh and non-negotiable alternatives' and which entails the call for a 'final decision', that is, the choice between clear alternatives to resolve the crisis. When the alternatives

---

1   R. Koselleck, 'Crisis' [1982], *Journal of the History of Ideas* 67:2 (2006), p. 399.

appear arbitrary – that is, when they do not allow a genuine choice between real, contrasting options – the possibility of a final decision is also lost: no decision that originates from the crisis is conclusive. Koselleck holds that, of abilities of the crisis to propose alternatives leading to a final decision – which led to its concept being interchangeable with those of 'conflict' and 'revolution' – only the ability to create ambivalence and connections remains: 'Not only can "crisis" be conjoined with other terms, it is easy to do so. While it can be used to clarify, all such coinages then require clarification. "Crisis" is often used interchangeably with "unrest", "conflict", "revolution", and to describe vaguely disturbing moods or situations. Every one of such uses is ambivalent.'[2] If the capacity of crisis to create connections and ambivalence no longer implies clearly discerning and discriminating between the alternatives that arise, then it can be modified according to its particular applications and to other concepts which may be linked with it, without limiting it to any particular meaning. But if this is the case, can it still properly be considered a concept?

I would argue that the current diffusion and pervasiveness of the term 'crisis' might be more than a sign of semantic vagueness. Koselleck argues that 'the term never crystallized into a concept sufficiently clear to be used as a basic concept in social, economic, or political language, despite – or perhaps because of – its manifold meanings'.[3] Indeed, the term 'crisis' acquires vagueness precisely when it is treated as a concept. Koselleck does exactly this when he poses questions about the concept of crisis such as 'What is it, what does it mean?' But in *this*

---

2   Ibid.
3   Ibid., p. 367.

crisis, we do not see the characteristics that Gilles Deleuze and Félix Guattari argue contribute to the definition of 'concept'. Although a concept is a compound of heterogeneous elements, it is nonetheless defined as 'the point of coincidence, condensation or accumulation of its own components'.[4] It follows, therefore, that the concept 'posits itself in itself – it is a self-positing'; it 'relates back to other concepts'; outside of the ambit of concepts 'it has no reference: it is self-referential'; it is 'incorporeal'.[5] In other words, the concept of crisis would be the acquired meaning of crisis – or 'created' meaning, as Deleuze and Guattari put it – that composed its elements. But the current crisis, although able to create links and ambivalences between elements, does not have a meaning responsible for their disposition. In short, this crisis poses heterogeneous elements without positing itself in itself, that is, without positing its own meaning. It always refers to the heterogeneous conditions that produced it, but the elements that it arranges are not exclusively of a conceptual nature; it directly affects people's lives, even in their most immediate corporal aspect. It thus acts as a *dispositif*.

The vagueness of this crisis considered as a concept gives it *its highest effectiveness as a dispositif*. Thus, to recognize the peculiarities of the current crisis and to understand the reasons for its effectiveness, I intend to investigate it in the same way one would investigate a *dispositif*, asking the question 'how does crisis work, what is its function?' Deleuze and Guattari's notion of a concept seems to overlap with that of a *dispositif*, but this overlapping also enables us to highlight the differences between

---

4 G. Deleuze and F. Guattari, *What is Philosophy?*, New York: Columbia University Press, 1994 [1991], p. 20.

5 Ibid., pp. 11, 19, 22, 21.

the two notions. My use of '*dispositif*' – or 'apparatus', as the French term is sometimes translated – refers to the definition provided by Michel Foucault, who introduced the term into the philosophical lexicon, making it essential to the understanding of a number of contemporary phenomena:

> What I'm trying to pick out with this term is, firstly, a thoroughly heterogeneous ensemble consisting of discourses, institutions, architectural forms, regulatory decisions, laws, administrative measures, scientific statements, philosophical, moral and philanthropic propositions – in short, the said as much as the unsaid. Such are the elements of the apparatus. The apparatus itself is the system of relations that can be established between these elements. Secondly, what I am trying to identify in this apparatus is precisely the nature of the connection that can exist between these heterogeneous elements. Thus, a particular discourse can figure at one time as the programme of an institution, and at another it can function as a means of justifying or masking a practice which itself remains silent, or as a secondary re-interpretation of this practice, opening out for it a new field of rationality. In short, between these elements, whether discursive or non-discursive, there is a sort of interplay of shifts of position and modifications of function which can also vary very widely.[6]

So, the ability of the term 'crisis' to create 'connections', to build a 'system of relations' among heterogeneous elements, finds its peculiar connotation not in a concept but in the form of a *dispositif*.

---

6   M. Foucault, 'The Confession of the Flesh', in *Power/Knowledge: Selected Interviews and Other Writings 1972–1977*, New York: Pantheon Books, 1980, pp. 194–5.

According to Foucault, the configuration of the crisis as *dispositif* also implies that the relationship established has 'a dominant strategic function'. That is, it creates 'relations of forces', a 'play of power':

> Thirdly, I understand by the term 'apparatus' a sort of – shall we say – formation which has as its major function at a given historical moment that of responding to an urgent need. The apparatus thus has a dominant strategic function ... I said that the apparatus is essentially of a strategic nature, which means assuming that it is a matter of a certain manipulation of relations of forces, either developing them in a particular direction, blocking them, stabilising them, utilising them, etc.[7]

The 'order of power' that makes use of *dispositifs* responds to an urgent need; as we will see, both as the 'programme of an institution' and as an internal 'means of justifying or masking', the *dispositif* acts to 'govern' that need. Finally, the 'play of power' in which the *dispositif* is inscribed involves, at the same time, a *limitation* in the possibility of fully grasping it in knowledge, or better, in a *certain* knowledge: 'The apparatus is thus always inscribed in a play of power, but it is also always linked to certain coordinates of knowledge which issue from it but, to an equal degree, condition it. This is what the apparatus consists in: strategies of relations of forces supporting, and supported by, types of knowledge.'[8]

In the course of this book, I will discuss all of these characteristics of the term 'dispositif' in more depth. However, even

---

7   Ibid., pp. 195–6.
8   Ibid., p. 196.

from this first articulation of its functions, it should be evident that the crisis we are experiencing assumes the features of a *dispositif*. Analysing the Foucauldian notion of *dispositif*, Deleuze uses the word 'crisis' to define that urgent need to which the *dispositif* responds: 'what is a *dispositif*? In the first instance it is above all a tangle, a multilinear ensemble. It is composed of lines, each having a different nature ... It is always in a crisis that Foucault discovers new dimensions, new lines.'[9] Crisis as *dispositif* is a certain disposition of a tangle of lines – which, as we have pointed out, are not simply of a conceptual nature but are of various different types – that intertwine in a certain historical conjuncture or, to use Deleuze's term, in 'the current':

> In each apparatus [*dispositif*] it is necessary to distinguish what we are (what we are already no longer), and what we are in the process of becoming: *the historical part and the current part* ... [T]he disciplines which Foucault describes are the history of what we gradually cease to be, and our present-day reality takes on the forms of dispositions of overt and continuous *control* in a way which is very different from recent closed disciplines.[10]

These 'dispositions of overt and continuous *control*', which appear in the current crisis, also activate Deleuzean lines of escape from the disciplinary society of the modern era and create the possibility of the new. This Deleuzean conception of the *dispositif* can make the processes of subjectification produced by the 'governmental' function of the *dispositif* of the crisis 'reversible'.[11]

---

9   G. Deleuze, 'What Is a Dispositif?', in *Michel Foucault Philosopher*, New York: Routledge, 1992, p. 159.

10   Ibid., p. 164.

11   Sandro Chignola insists on the 'ever bilateral and reversible' aspect

In Foucault, however, the *dispositifs* of overt and continuous control – those of a medico-legal nature which he takes as a model in the interview I quote above – operate primarily in their ruling function to give order to that tangle of lines of which the *dispositif* is composed. Giorgio Agamben's reading of the term *dispositif* – which also derives from Foucault – moves in that direction: 'Further expanding the already large class of Foucauldian apparatuses, I shall call an apparatus literally anything that has in some way the capacity to capture, orient, determine, intercept, model, control, or secure the gestures, behaviors, opinions, or discourses of living beings.'[12]

It is in this sense that the recent crisis operates as a *dispositif*. Since it essentially establishes a certain power relation, it today carries out that function which marks it as the art of government par excellence. The dominant form of power and the process of subjectification that it activates can be defined through analysis of how this crisis currently works, and of how it arranges heterogeneous elements to order its discourse. If we look at the legal sense of the term *dispositif* emphasized by Agamben, crisis ' "is the part of a judgment that contains the decision separate from the opinion". That is, the section of a sentence that decides, or the enacting clause of a law.'[13] While the modern

of the *dispositif* when comparing Foucault, Deleuze and Agamben. See S. Chignola, 'Sul dispositivo. Foucault, Agamben, Deleuze', in *Da dentro. Biopolitica, bioeconomia, Italian Theory*, Rome: DeriveApprodi, 2018, pp. 173–90. For a different genealogy of the *dispositif*, based on Canguilhem's, also challenging Agamben's interpretation, see M. Pasquinelli, 'Che cosa (non) è un dispositivo. Sull'archeologia della norma in Canguilhem, Foucault e Agamben', in D. Gentili and E. Stimilli (eds.), *Differenze italiane. Politica e filosofia: mappe e sconfinamenti*, Rome: DeriveApprodi, 2015, pp. 184–99.

12   G. Agamben, 'What Is an Apparatus?', in *What Is an Apparatus and Other Essays*, Stanford: Stanford University Press, 2009, p. 14.

13   Ibid., p. 7.

concept of crisis was the expression of an order of power which had the meaning of 'final decision and resolution', as a juridical *dispositif*, crisis consists in the judgment as provision and not in the decision as a resolution of the crisis itself.

The question to be asked, then, concerns the order of power within which crisis is configured as a *dispositif*. The fact that the current crisis cannot be resolved could be considered a sign of its lack of effectiveness in the context of the modern order of power, while it is anything but ineffective if it is considered within another order of power, that of neoliberal capitalism. Marx had already defined capital as a relation, a 'social relation', therefore we could say that even for Marx capital *tout court* works by its very nature through what we now call *dispositifs*. Neoliberalism, however, marked its discontinuity from the modern capitalism of Marx's day by acquiring a biopolitical dimension. In contemporary society and capitalist modes of production, neoliberalism determines a biopolitical order, an order in which – as we shall see – the alternatives produced involve decisions which are neither final nor definitive, but are functional to the government of the lives that take shape within it. Thus, it can be argued that the current crisis configures itself according to a biopolitical paradigm, and that the precariat which is today characterized in terms of so-called 'human resources' is the form of life that has emerged from it. This book will articulate these initial assumptions through a genealogy of the function of the 'art of government' of the crisis, a function that currently makes it one of the most efficient and effective biopolitical *dispositifs* of neoliberalism.

2
The Forensic Judgment

The Court

The criteria with which we define crisis today differ from the modern paradigm of crisis. However, this does not mean that these criteria are entirely new. In fact, as we shall see, today more than ever crisis is configured around traits that make it much closer to its original formula than to that of modernity. I therefore want to return to the semantic range of the word 'crisis' and to the complexity produced by its Greek etymology. In Greek, *krisis* means 'distinctive force, separation, division', but also 'decision, resolution, judgment, election, choice'. Considering this semantic constellation allows us to outline the configuration of crisis: its meaning does not derive from privileging one sense over the other, but from the way in which they are arranged, and from the order which they together constitute. The *dispositif* of crisis operates so as to 'divide and distinguish' its own elements, so that this 'distinction' offers an alternative. This alternative proposes a 'choice' that is an important and constitutive element of crisis itself, rather than a 'decision' that intervenes from the outside to resolve the crisis and find a way out of it. Thus, crisis is a mode of judgment that does not provide for a 'final decision'; rather, the choice is resolved within the crisis, meaning that the crisis as such is not subject to judgment. In short, crisis is not what is judged, but is rather the mode of judging. This is the meaning of 'judgment' suggested by the semantic spectrum of crisis, as it emerges in the different fields and contexts in which the *dispositif* is active.

In ancient Greece, the term *krisis* was most frequently used in the medical and political fields. Let us start from its use in politics or, to be more precise, in the political-legal field. We have to go back to Aristotle – as Koselleck does – to determine the political-legal use of *krisis*, particularly to some passages from *Politics*. For instance, this line from the beginning of *Politics*: 'Justice on the other hand is an element of the state; for judicial procedure, which means the decision (*krisis*) of what is just, is the regulation (*taxis*) of the political partnership.'[1] This appears only a few lines after Aristotle's famous definition of man as 'by nature a political animal'[2] who is, by nature, inclined to live in a community. It follows that, as a community par excellence, the polis exists 'by nature': 'Hence every city-state exists by nature, inasmuch as the first partnerships so exist; for the city-state is the end of the other partnerships, and nature is an end.'[3] Therefore, *krisis* acquires its peculiar function within an order whose origin is 'by nature'; it does not determine the order, but it is one of the elements that contributes to its regulation.

1   Aristotle, *Politics*, ed. J. Henderson, Cambridge, MA: Harvard University Press, 2005, p. 13 [1253a, 38–40].
2   Ibid., p. 9 [1253a, 3].
3   Ibid. [1252b, 31–3].

In fact, *krisis* does not decide about justice as such, but about its application in individual cases; it intervenes in these cases to judge 'what is just', which for Aristotle concerns the individual citizen of the polis. Crisis is therefore the principle of justice that is to be applied in each specific case: it intervenes in 'the regulation (*taxis*) of the political partnership' concerning the relations between individual citizens; however, the existence of a political partnership depends on the inclinations of human nature.

The 'decision' of *krisis* is therefore forced, and aimed at preserving the existing political order, which is associated with balance, harmony, and measurement – thus with *justice*. *Krisis* carries out this task in court, and its decision is 'judicial', since it enforces a rule and judges on a case-by-case basis. But who is in charge of enforcing justice, who is entrusted with the *krisis* within the polis? Aristotle leaves no room for doubt: *krisis* and *krinein* pertain to the art of government, and, therefore, to the duties of the rulers (*archontov*). In *Politics* again, the 'judgment' (*krisis*) is the prerogative of those who govern the city and, in particular, of those who must maintain and regulate its order: 'The activities of the state are those of the rulers (*archontov*) and those of the person ruled (*archomenon*), and the work of a ruler is to direct the administration (*epitaxis*) and to judge law-suits (*krisis*).'[4] The judgment of *krisis* is thus included in the administration of the polis and is not the 'political' decision resulting in the distinction between rulers and ruled, between those who act and those who are submitted to the *arche*. It does not concern the *arche* ('beginning', 'origin', 'guidance'), which refers to the 'guidance' and 'direction' in the political sense of the government of the polis. The judgment of crisis is the art

---

4   Ibid., pp. 557–9 [1326b, 12–14].

of government understood as *epitaxis* ('disposition', 'organization', 'order'), which is a tool for the preservation of the existing order. It pertains to the administration of the polis and does not define *who* rules and who does not. Therefore, crisis is a mode of *judgment*, not in the sense of 'political decision', but as endorsement, validation, legitimacy, the preservation of a certain political order or condition which has its own set of rules. As was already the case in Plato's *Laws*, for Aristotle the 'judgment' defined by *krisis* is properly 'judicial' and has to be pronounced, among the rulers, by the judges of the polis: 'What constitutes a citizen is therefore clear from these considerations: we now declare that one who has the right to participate in deliberative or judicial (*kritiches*) office is a citizen of the state in which he has that right, and a state is a collection of such persons sufficiently numerous, speaking broadly, to secure independence of life.'[5] *Krisis* is therefore announced not to establish an order, but to enforce it. In other words, it must be assumed that the order is already given.

The Aristotelian sense of *krisis* – on which the history of the concept usually relies – confirms the acquisition of its meaning in the sphere of the administration of justice, but the 'technical' definition of *krisis* as 'judicial deliberation' has wider implications. In Parmenides' poem *On Nature*, we find the model of the judgment of *krisis* to be a proposition fundamental to the whole of Western thought: 'justice (*Dike*) doth not lose her fetters and let anything come into being or pass away, but holds it fast. Our judgment (*krisis*) thereon depends on this: "Is it or is it not?" Surely it is adjudged, as it needs must be (*ananke*), that we are to set aside the one way as unthinkable and nameless (for it is

---

5   Ibid., p. 179 [1275b, 17–21].

no true way), and that the other path is real and true.'[6] Despite the fact that there is a long and dominant philosophical tradition of placing Parmenides' discourse on an ontological plane, this fragment should also be read on the political-judicial level. For, in the Greek world, the two planes overlap. It is worth remembering that the analogy between the judicial and the 'natural' dimensions is typical of pre-Socratic thought. Not only is this apparent with regards to justice (*dike*), but the very idea of *cosmos* ascribes to nature an order which is judicial in origin:

> there is an even earlier reflection of the ideal of law, in the work of the natural philosopher Anaximander of Miletus, about the middle of the sixth century. Transferring the concept of *dike* from the social life of the city-state to the realm of nature, he explains the causal connection between coming-to-be and passing-away as equivalent to a lawsuit, in which things are compelled by the decision of Time to compensate each other for their unrighteousness. This is the origin of the philosophical idea of *cosmos*: for the word originally signifies the *right order* in a state or other community.[7]

To correspond to necessity, justice must assume the features of the 'lawsuit', both in the polis and in the cosmos. I will now delve more deeply into an analysis of *krisis* and its determination.

One element is clear: the decision of *krisis* is dictated by necessity. Justice corresponds precisely with Necessity: *Dike* is *Ananke*. In deciding between two alternative ways – only one of which is true, while the other simply 'is not', or is a

6   Parmenides, *On Nature*, in J. Burnet (ed.), *Early Greek Philosophy*, London: A & C Black, 1920, pp. 129–30 [Fragment 8].

7   W. Jaeger, *Paideia: The Ideals of Greek Culture*, Vol. I, Oxford: Basil Blackwell, 1946, p. 110.

'non-way' – the judgment and the decision of *krisis* are predetermined by justice. In other words, they are 'necessitated' by
justice: *krisis* is a decision, but it is a forced one. Plato made a
radical break with this approach, which could be understood to
represent one of the elements of that well-known philosophical (and political) 'parricide' committed against Parmenides.
Plato separated justice from its 'judicial' meaning and this relation with necessity, and turned it into a pre-eminently 'political'
question.

It is in the *Republic* that the judgment of *krisis* acquires that
particular meaning that, with Aristotle, became paradigmatic.
The way in which *krisis* enters the discussion in the *Republic*
makes clear its political function, which Aristotle adopted in the
passages of *Politics* mentioned above, in which he only defines
the 'use' and 'application' of *krisis* within the order of the polis.
Aristotle thus inherited from Plato the idea that *krisis* is not
the judgment establishing or expressing justice: such judgment
is, instead, truly 'political', while *krisis* has a merely 'judicial'
sense. We must therefore trace the necessary character of *krisis*
that derives from Parmenides back to this 'judicial' sense: *krisis*
expresses a judgment that leads unequivocally to forced decisions. I will now follow Plato's argument step by step.

It is no accident that *krisis* appears in the Platonic dialogue
when the interlocutors are debating justice, wondering whether
or not it is good to be just, and discussing the criteria to use
in order to discriminate between the just and the unjust man.
Glaucon, Socrates' interlocutor, is speaking. He argues:

> But to come now to the decision (*krisin*) between our two kinds of
> life, if we separate the most completely just and the most completely

unjust man, we shall be able to decide (*krinai*) rightly, but if not, not. How, then, is this separation to be made? Thus: we must subtract nothing of his injustice from the unjust man or of his justice from the just, but assume the perfection of each in his own mode of conduct.[8]

The judgment of *krisis* then involves a 'confrontation' between two terms – in this case, the ways of life of the just and the unjust man. To produce a correct judgment, that is, in order for the decision to be right in the sense of 'justness', the chasm must be 'extreme'. The confrontation must, in other words, propose an alternative.

However, just a few lines suffice to show that this criterion is not conclusive. It does not lead to the determination of what justice is; on the contrary, it suggests that it is not 'good' to be just and that living as unjust men might be more advantageous for leading a happy life. Socrates, however, responds to his interlocutor ironically, suggesting that the criterion of *krisis* is neither suitable for establishing what justice is, nor does it lead to respect for justice: "'Bless me, my dear Glaucon," said I, "how strenuously you polish them up for the decision (*krisin*), first one and then the other, as if they were two statues!'"[9] The dialogue thus abandons the method of *krisis*, which cannot establish the nature of justice, and, instead, focuses on the foundation of a polis whose principle – *arche* – is justice. In other words, *krisis* does not decide on the principle of justice, but presupposes it in order to be able to correctly judge in disputes 'between individuals', in order, as in Aristotle, to be able to

8 Plato, *Republic*, ed. J. Henderson, Cambridge, MA: Harvard University Press, 1937, p. 121 [II, 360e].
9 Ibid., p. 362 [II, 361d] (translation modified).

apply justice in each case. This is why the question of what justice is cannot be reduced to discriminating between righteous and unrighteous isolated individuals: 'Then, perhaps, there would be more justice in the larger object and more easy to apprehend. If it please you, then, let us first look for its quality in states, and then only examine it also in the individual, looking for the likeness of the greater in the form of the less.'[10]

For Plato's Socrates, *krisis* can effectively discriminate what is just from what is unjust only within a polis already founded on justice. Only the city founded on justice is always capable of 'good counsel', because, in this way, judgment is based on science (*episteme*) and wisdom (*sophia*). This is not the judgment of *krisis*, however, but that of *euboulia*, which expresses the will of the assembly (*boule*) of citizens, whose decision is right *because it is the result of common debate*. Only the judgment produced and shared in the assembly involves men as living beings rather than 'statues'. *Boulesis* is the mode of judgment peculiar to the way of life par excellence, that is, to political life. As a properly political decision, *boulesis* cannot be reduced to the judgment of *krisis*: it is decision without judgment.

Therefore, because it is peculiar to political life, 'good counsel' is not determined by its content – what justice is, what distinguishes between the just and the unjust – but by the way in which judgment is reached: 'And surely this very thing, good counsel, is a form of wisdom. For it is not by ignorance but by knowledge that men counsel well.'[11] Justice therefore corresponds to the well governed city; it is only by living in a well-governed polis that the individual citizen can be considered

---

10   Ibid., p. 369 [II, 369a].
11   Ibid., p. 349 [IV, 428b].

just or unjust, and it is only within such a polis that *krisis* finds its place for legitimately formulating its judgment: the 'court', where Aristotle places *krisis* without further explanation about the nature of its judgment.

In short, it is not the court that creates justice, but vice versa: it is justice that creates the court. Justice gives the measure – 'justness' – to the judgment of *krisis*, to the judicial decision of the court. *Krisis* does not produce justice but presupposes it.

In *The Statesman*, Plato is equally explicit in limiting the judgment of *krisis* to 'righteous judges', without making it a prerogative of the politician; indeed, in order for their judgment to be correct, it must be limited to the 'enactments' of the king legislator and to the administration of his power, certainly not extending to its institution and constitution, which must remain the prerogative of the sovereign, the *basileus*. Therefore, despite his disillusionment about the future of the democratic polis, which, by then, had already been compromised, Plato retains the view already expressed in the *Republic*, that *krisis* only concerns the judgment about 'contracts' among individuals and does not concern 'political art', which is the responsibility of those who rule the polis, and specifically consists in drawing 'them together by friendship and community of sentiment into a common life'.[12] As in Aristotle, *krisis* is at the service of the 'rulers':

---

12 Plato, *The Statesman*, ed. J. Henderson, Cambridge, MA: Harvard University Press, 2006, p. 195 [311, c1]. Foucault refers to this and other passages of *The Stateman* to show how, in the Greek world – with the significant exception of Pythagoras' texts – political power did not take the form of the pastorate as 'individualizing power': 'Plato did admit that the physician, the farmer, the gymnasiarch, and the pedagogue acted as shepherds. But he refused to get them involved with the politician's activity … [T]he men who hold political power are not to be shepherds. Their task doesn't consist in

Stranger – Has it [the power of righteous judges] any power beyond that of judging men's contracts with one another, pronouncing (*krinein*) them right or wrong by the standard of the existing laws which it has received from the king and law-giver, showing its own peculiar virtue in that it is not so perverted by any bribes, or fears, or pity, or enmity, or friendship, as ever to consent to decide the lawsuits of men with each other contrary to the enactments (*taxin*) of the law-giver?

Socrates – No; the business of this power is about as you have described it.

Stranger – Then we find that the strength of judges is not kingly, but is guardian of laws and a servant (*yperetin*) of the kingly power.[13]

The Last Judgment

The court's mode of judgment was made into the 'supreme, definitive, final judgment' by Christianity. The judgment of *krisis* became a paradigm for the Last Judgment, which would discriminate between the just and the unjust. The Last Judgment has an analogy in Plato, in the myth told by Socrates in *Gorgias*. The setting is once again a court, and the judgment is that of *krisis*, which must discriminate between those who were just and those who were unjust, assigning to each one either the reward of the island of the blessed or condemnation to Tartarus:

---

fostering the life of a group of individuals. It consists in forming and assuring the city's unity.' M. Foucault, 'Omnes et Singulatim: Towards a Criticism of "Political Reason"' [1979], in *Power: Essential Works of Michel Foucault 1954–1984*, Vol. 3, New York: The New Press, 2000, p. 307.

13   Plato, *The Statesman*, p. 173 [305, b-c].

Now in the time of Cronos there was a law concerning mankind, and it holds to this very day amongst the gods, that every man who has passed a just and holy life departs after his decease to the Isles of the Blest, and dwells in all happiness apart from ill; but whoever has lived unjustly and impiously goes to the dungeon of requital and penance which, you know, they call Tartarus. Of these men there were judges in Cronos' time, and when Zeus had but newly begun his reign – living men to judge the living upon the day when each was to breathe his last; and thus the cases were being decided amiss ... Then spake Zeus: 'Nay', said he, 'I will put a stop to these proceedings. The cases are now indeed judged ill; and it is because they who are on trial are tried in their clothing, for they are tried alive. Now many', said he, 'who have wicked souls are clad in fair bodies and ancestry and wealth, and at their judgement (*krisis*) appear many witnesses to testify that their lives have been just. Now, the judges are confounded not only by their evidence but at the same time by being clothed themselves while they sit in judgement, having their own soul muffled in the veil of eyes and ears and the whole body. Thus all these are a hindrance to them, their own habiliments no less than those of the judged ... [T]hey must be stripped bare of all those things before they are tried; for they must stand their trial dead. Their judge also must be naked, dead, beholding with very soul the very soul of each immediately upon his death, bereft of all his kin and having left behind on earth all that fine array, to the end that the judgement (*krisis*) may be just.'[14]

Although the context differs from that of the *Republic*, the question is the same: what criterion should be used to judge

---

14   Plato, *Gorgias*, ed. J. Henderson, Cambridge, MA: Harvard University Press, 2006, pp. 519–21 [523, b–e].

and discriminate between the just and the unjust? This comple-
ments rather than contradicts its determination in the *Republic*,
in which the mode of judgment of *krisis* is effective only if
every individual under judgment is 'polished up as if he were
a statue'. In *Gorgias*, in order for the judgment of *krisis* to be
performed in a manner appropriate to its peculiar mode, men
should not be 'tried in their clothing', that is, in the bodies and
forms of life of their earthly existence. When judged, they
should not be 'alive', but 'naked' and 'dead'. The judge must
be naked and dead as well, and his judgment mustn't be dis-
tracted by the 'array' of the earthly life of the judged. Only in
this way can *krisis* discriminate and express itself in absolute
terms either for or against.

Christianity elevated the judgment of *krisis* – which expresses
two mutually exclusive absolute alternatives – to the judgment
par excellence. It is present not only in the Final Judgment at the
end of time, but also in 'divine judgment' which, intervening in
history, from time to time confers meaning on its events and its
trajectory.[15] This secularization and historicization of the divine
judgment is the presupposition of that political theology which,
by analogy, assumes *krisis* as a paradigm of political decision.

However, even in *Gorgias*, Plato does not foresee this
outcome. *Krisis* does indeed take the form of the last judgment,
but to do so it cannot apply to living beings or to their earthly

---

15   Analysing how the fall of the Roman Empire, and hence the end
of the ancient world, was interpreted in the different epochs, Santo Mazzarino found that during the Middle Ages, and in particular by Augustine and
his followers, decline and decadence were seen as signs of the 'judgment of
God', whereas they were originally considered part of the natural and organic
process of aging. See S. Mazzarino, *The End of the Ancient World*, New York:
Knopf, 1966.

activity and particularities, nor to their political life. The judgment typical of political life is never structured as an irreducible alternative. Political judgment is not the outcome of a process, but the process itself:[16] it is the *way* in which a resolution is reached, and not the particular content of the resolution, which in its particularity and contingency can be either right or wrong. Even if a given deliberation proved in fact to be wrong, this would not at all invalidate the justice from which it proceeded, which is nothing but the collective practice of *boule*. The judgment of *krisis* therefore does not correspond to the highest form of judgment, because the latter should correspond to the highest form of life, that is, to political life: 'And afterwards, having practised it [virtue] together, we shall in due course, if we deem it right, embark on politics, or proceed to consult on whatever we may think fit, being then better equipped for such counsel (*bouleustai*) than we are now.'[17] Virtue is an exercise that concerns the individual, who will be judged on a case-by-case basis and then rewarded or condemned. Yet, although individual virtue contributes to making better collective decisions, political decision should be placed on another level: that of political life.

---

16 Nicole Loraux traces the etymology of the word *agorà* to the meaning of 'process', the *agon* of conflicting opinions, whose case is however not legal, but political. See N. Loraux, *The Divided City: On Memory and Forgetting in Ancient Athens*, New York: Zone Books, 2006.

17 Plato, *Gorgias*, pp. 531–3 [527, d].

3
The Medical Judgment

Hippocrates: Servant of the Polis

The forensic sense of *krisis* is similar to its medical meaning – or, better, the 'judicial' meaning that *krisis* has in politics corresponds to its use in the medical field. Indeed, *krisis* as judgment that reduces the terms of the decision to an absolute alternative finds its paradigm in the judgment on the life and death of a diseased patient. Once the disease causes an imbalance in the body, *krisis* intervenes to 'diagnose' the course to be followed in order to stabilize its vital functions and restore health: diagnosis and prognosis, *discernment* and *judgment*. In short, *krisis* determines *how* a given disease will evolve: its course either towards death or salvation. This is not a decision about life and death, but the 'diagnosis' of a natural phenomenon. Just like in politics, in medicine *krisis* can judge between the extremes of life and death because it presupposes an order – the natural and organic order – that is not produced by the judgment. It is not the medical judgment that produces health, but the evolution of the disease towards recovery that indicates the judgment to the physician.

In the medical field, the main point of reference is Hippocrates and his school, whose teaching has been handed down to us through Galen. As is well known, the latter was influenced by Aristotle (who, in his turn, was the son of a physician). Taking this argument step by step, we will first explore the meaning attributed to *krisis* by Hippocrates. For him, as for Aristotle and Plato, crisis meant 'judgment': 'Life is short, the Art long, opportunity (*kairos*) fleeting, experience treacherous, judgment (*krisis*) difficult.'[1] The judgment that crisis determines consists in the diagnosis of healing – in the discernment of the evolution towards a return to health. Crisis, usually preceded by the worsening of a fever, corresponded to the period in which it was possible for the physician to diagnose healing and to make a prognosis that, if the same symptoms were to return on the same dates in the year and in the same circumstances, the disease would progress again in the same manner. It was in the prognosis in particular that the physician performed their art. For the process of healing depended solely on nature and, in order for it to be 'perfect' and complete, had to come from within, through the actions of the body itself. External intervention, when really necessary, was to be as limited as possible.[2] Nature took its course, while the physician had to recognize the symptoms of

---

1   Hippocrates, 'Aphorisms', in *Hippocrates*, Vol. IV, ed. W.H.S. Jones, Cambridge, MA: Harvard University Press, 1957, p. 99.

2   In the treatment of diseases, Plato is in line with Hippocrates and his school: 'Further, as concerns the motions, the best motion of a body is that caused by itself in itself; for this is most nearly akin to the motion of intelligence and the motion of the Universe ... With respect to the structure of diseases also the same rule holds good: whenever anyone does violence thereto by drugging, in despite of the predestined period of time, diseases many and grave, in place of few and slight, are wont to occur'. Plato, *Timaeus*, ed. J. Henderson, Cambridge, MA: Harvard University Press, 2005, pp. 243–5.

the recovery and diagnose the crisis: 'Coctions signify near-
ness of crisis and surety of recovery, but raw and unconcocted
evacuations and those that turn into bad abscessions signify
absence of crisis, pain, prolongation, death, or a relapse of the
same symptoms. But which of these results is most likely, you
must investigate on the basis of other signs. Declare the past,
diagnose the present, foretell the future; practice these acts.'[3]

The role of the physician is one of the three moments of
the art of medicine. The physician was neither its ruler nor
master, but, as the term *yperetes* indicates, its 'servant': 'The
art has three factors, the disease, the patient, the physician. The
physician is the servant (*yperetes*) of the art. The patient must
co-operate with the physician in combating the disease.'[4] The
analogy with the function of *krisis* in the forensic field is evident
from the use of the term *yperetes*. As we have seen, Plato uses
the same term in *The Statesman*, when he defines the judge as 'a
servant (*yperetes*) of the kingly power', thus restricting judicial
power in relation to political power. *Krisis* is the expression of
a condition – justice or health – which is considered vital and
to be the product of a natural inclination. Those who exercise
the judgment of *krisis* – those who administrate the polis or
who are the 'servants' of the medical art – derive their authority
from the order they have to enforce or re-establish, and which
they serve.[5] However, although the physician does not play a

---

3   Hippocrates, 'Epidemics I', in *Hippocrates*, Vol. I, ed. W.H.S. Jones,
Cambridge, MA: Harvard University Press, 1957, p. 163–5. 'Coction' is a
change in the humours during disease.

4   Ibid.

5   In this way Hippocrates refers to Abderites, who had asked for his
intervention to cure Democritus' madness: 'I, convinced that science is the
gift of the gods, and that men are the works of Nature (take no offence,
Abderites), believe that not you, but Nature herself is calling me to save her

decisive role when nature has to take its course, he is called upon to exercise his art when it comes to 'epidemics', that is, when the disease acts – literally: *epi-demos* – 'on the population', in other words, on the natural life of the *demos*, and affects the individual as part of this population: 'Diseases from nature, nature herself judges (brings to a crisis) and heals. Those from a visitation [of the plague epidemics] the science heals, judging scientifically the alterations of bodies. Hippocrates the physician cures this malady.'[6]

Hippocrates' description of the population as the subject of epidemics resembles that which Foucault gives in 1977, when he defines epidemics as the new subject-object of the biopolitical art of government, that is, of 'governmentality'. Foucault also claims that the concept of the population as a figure that is different from the people began to take shape – among other events that characterized the transition to modernity – with the great epidemics of the seventeenth and eighteenth centuries. The spread of diseases beyond the boundaries of the nation-state led to the delineation and defining of a figure – the population – that could not be reduced to the political and legal paradigms of sovereignty and the people. If epidemics anticipated this supra-state of 'globalization', the population was its subject from the beginning. Unlike the people, the population cannot be defined through the command-obedience constraint

_____

creation which is in danger of crumbling through disease. Hence instead of you I now obey Nature and the gods' command to heal the ailing Democritus.' Hippocrates, *Pseudepigraphic Writings: Letters – Embassy – Speech from the Altar – Decree*, ed. W.D. Smith, Leiden: Brill, 1990, p. 59. These *epistoles* of Hippocrates are now considered apocryphal, but they belong nevertheless to the *Corpus Hippocraticum*.

6   Ibid., p. 49.

imposed by the sovereign contract and regulated by the artifice of law, but begins to assume its own shape only in the moment in which it is considered to be in some ways 'natural':

> [Population] will be considered as a set of processes to be managed at the level and on the basis of what is natural in these processes. But what does this 'naturalness' of the population signify? What is it that means that the population will henceforth be seen, not from the standpoint of the juridical-political notion of subject, but as a sort of technical-political object of management and government? ... In fact, the population is not a primary datum; it is dependent on a series of variables. Population varies with the climate. It varies with the material surroundings. It varies with the intensity of commerce and activity in the circulation of wealth. Obviously it varies according to the laws to which it is subjected ... It also varies with people's customs ... Population varies with the moral or religious values associated with different kinds of conduct ... Above all, of course, it varies with the condition of means of subsistence ... [T]he population is not that kind of original datum, that kind of material on which the sovereign's action is to be exercised, that vis-à-vis of the sovereign.[7]

The population that the epidemics of the seventeenth and eighteenth centuries began to shape is primarily the object of medical knowledge, and only indirectly the responsibility of the sovereign. In the same period, it also became the object of economic knowledge, which had to deal with the problem of the lack of grain to fulfil the needs of the European market.

---

7   M. Foucault, *Security, Territory, Population: Lectures at the Collège de France, 1977–1978*, ed. M. Senellart, London: Palgrave Macmillan, 2009, pp. 70–1.

Thus, medicine and economy end up sharing the same *dispositif* of government because they have the same object: the population. The 'naturalness' of the population refers both to medicine and economy. Later, 'taking care' of the population became the concern of politics, in that art of government which we call 'biopolitics'. It was, therefore, the synergy of medicine and economy in respectively addressing epidemics and the scarcity of grain that laid the foundation for biopolitics.[8]

When analysing the causes of the outbreak and spread of epidemics, Hippocrates attributes aspects that are not exclusively organic to the 'naturalness' of the *demos*. The capability of his 'art of medicine' to intervene, therefore, does not depend on diseases that are derived from nature, because, as we have seen, 'nature herself judges (brings to a crisis) and heals'. It depends, instead, on the prescriptive and disciplining aspect of prognosis. Indeed, epidemics are caused and spread not only as a result of strictly physiological aspects (concerning the individual's body), but also due to specific geographic, territorial and climatic conditions, as well as equally relevant factors such as the political regime and customs and individual and collective traditions. From a medical point of view, therefore, epidemics define a *demos* that is not *politeia*, that is, not the political community of the polis. It is, rather, 'population'. If, therefore, nature itself leads to crisis and heals individuals, and if political *techne* governs the citizens of the polis, it follows that population – as a group of individuals united by more than just the fact of being

---

8 'For capitalist society, it was biopolitics, the biological, the somatic, the corporal, that mattered more than anything else. The body is a biopolitical reality; medicine is a biopolitical strategy.' M. Foucault, 'The Birth of Social Medicine' [1977], in *Power: The Essential Works of Michel Foucault 1954–1984*, Vol. 2, ed. J. Faubion, London: Allen Lane, 2000, p. 137.

part of the same political community – is a peculiar product of the medical *techne*. Without taking the analogy too far, it is clear that the characteristics of the *demos* subjected to the epidemic defined by Hippocrates seem to correspond to those of the 'population' that Foucault derives from treatises on the seventeenth- and eighteenth-century epidemics, through which he elaborates his conception of biopolitics and governmentality. At work in both cases, indeed, is the same *dispositif* of the 'naturalization' of traits that are not immediately 'natural' – but rather social, political, cosmological, and behavioural. Strictly physiological aspects are therefore listed along with others that are 'cultural':

> The following were the circumstances attending the diseases, from which I framed my judgments, learning from the common nature of all and the particular nature of the individual, from the disease, the patient, the regimen prescribed and the prescriber – for these make a diagnosis more favourable or less; from the constitution, both as a whole and with respect to the parts, of the weather and of each region; from the custom, mode of life, practices and ages of each patient; from talk, manner, silence, thoughts, sleep or absence of sleep, the nature and time of dreams, pluckings, scratchings, tears; from the exacerbations, stools, urine, sputa, vomit, the antecedents and consequents of each member in the successions of diseases, and the abscessions to a fatal issue or a crisis, sweat, rigor, chill, cough, sneezes, hiccoughs, breathing, belchings, flatulence, silent or noisy, hemorrhages, and hemorrhoids. From these things must we consider what their consequents also will be.[9]

---

9 Hippocrates, 'Epidemics I', p. 181.

However, I am not arguing that there is a sort of biopolitics *ante litteram* in Hippocrates and in ancient medicine. It is true that, in the case of epidemics – that is, when the art of medicine proves most appropriate and effective – physicians carry out their duty fully: they 'govern' and 'administer' the hygiene and health of the population. But this art of governing the administration of health – medical prognosis – is not to be confused with the art of politics. Indeed, as we have learned from Plato and Aristotle, the judgment of the medical *techne* as *krisis* is similar to *krisis* in the judicial sphere, in the sense that it does not correspond to the judgment and the decision of political *techne*. It is therefore entirely inappropriate to speak of biopolitics with regard to the medical administration of the population as the subject of an epidemic. Yet, much later, it is precisely the blurring of the distinction between the medical and the political *techne* – and the subordination, established by Plato, of the former to the latter – that would turn crisis into an art of biopolitical government. Together, the medical *techne* and the judicial *techne* – to which, in the modern era, we must also add the economic *techne* – would configure the political *techne* in a biopolitical sense.

For Hippocrates, political power rules over the art of medicine. In fact, when Artaxerxes requested his services as a physician to heal the Persian army of an epidemic, Hippocrates answered in his capacity as a Greek citizen, rejecting the request on the basis of his political allegiance, which prevailed over the principles of his medical art: 'Send back to the king as quickly as possible that I have enough food, clothing, shelter and all substance sufficient for life, and I am unwilling to enjoy Persian opulence or to save Persians from disease, since they are enemies of the Greeks.'[10] Unlike Hippocrates, epidemics do not distinguish between friends and enemies, and neither is the political value of the population defined through the friend/enemy criterion. As we have seen in Foucault, only in the modern era would the biopolitical art of government start to take shape, working beyond the people and the state, and thus attributing to the population its own political connotation.

Galen: Between Life and Death

In the Hellenistic age, Galen deviated from Hippocrates' approach, to lessen the role of a natural inclination towards healing in the definition of crisis. It seems to be with his treatment of crisis that the term acquired the meaning of the 'condition of suspension between life and death' which can be found in early modern encyclopaedias and dictionaries. It was thanks to his teaching that the role attributed to the 'judgment' of the physician would become increasingly important in the definition of crisis. Of the elements that characterize Hippocrates' art of medicine, Galen focuses primarily on 'opportunity' (*kairos*), that is, the opportune moment for pronouncing the diagnosis.[11] In Galen, *kairos* becomes the moment when the subjectivity of the physician emerges through the decision. Unlike Hippocrates' cases, which focused on describing the patients' symptoms, Galen focuses instead on the physician's therapies.[12]

---

10   Hippocrates, *Pseudepigraphic Writings*, p. 53.

11   For a study of *kairos* as opportune moment, deriving from its meaning in ancient philosophy, see G. Marramao, *Kairós: Towards an Ontology of Due Time*, Aurora, CO: The Davies Group Publishers, 2006.

12   See S.P. Mattern, *Galen and the Rhetoric of Healing*, Baltimore: The Johns Hopkins University Press, 2008.

There is no *krisis* – whether the disease affects the individual or the population – that does not require medical examination. Although he does not put himself in the place of nature, the physician is nonetheless the one who knows how nature heals or, alternatively, how its propensity to the preservation of life can eventually succumb to the disease:

> Whether the crisis is a sudden change in the disease, or just the propensity toward a better condition, or an alteration that precedes these options, or any solution of the disease, or whether the crisis is only that which someone wants to call good, my only purpose here is not primarily to make the distinction, but, as someone who knows all these things properly, I decided to examine them. The best principle of their prognosis, which in fact also applies to the future, thus [crisis] is also called the most acute period of the entire disease.[13]

It is precisely the latter sense of crisis – 'the most acute period of the entire disease' – in which there is no sign of any natural inclination towards healing, which characterized its meaning in ancient medicine *tout court*. Crisis then means the struggle, the conflict between life and death, the outcome of which is uncertain.

Another aspect of ancient medicine's notion of crisis, which will become relevant for our discussion, is the close connection between the diagnosis and prognosis of crisis and the ancient astronomy of the Pythagorean system, which influenced both Hippocrates[14]

---

13   Galen, *Peri criseon*, L. I, c. 1 (translation by SP).
14   These are the words that Hippocrates writes to his son: 'And in relation to cycles, irrational alterations of revers, and crises of the ill, let orderly calculations assist for safety in disease.' Hippocrates, *Pseudepigraphic Writings*, p. 101.

and Galen.[15] The fact that recovering from illness – crisis – is
understood as a 'return' and as the 're-establishment' of the
initial health condition finds a close connection in the calculation of the 'revolutions' of the moon or other planets. This is not
merely an analogy: the 'critical' days of a disease and the course
of the crisis were in fact established on the basis of astronomical
calculations. Hippocrates agreed with Galen that, if the crisis
did not occur on the expected dates, the disease would evolve
for the worst, possibly leading to death: 'one must know that, if
the crises be on other days than the above, there will be relapses,
and there may also be a fatal issue. So one must be attentive
and know that at these times there will be the crises resulting in
recovery, or death, or a tendency for better or worse.'[16] It was
therefore the calendar – that is, the cosmic order – that decided
the outcome of the disease. Crisis as such was the time of the
diagnosis, not of the decision. At most, the diagnosis could make
use of the prognosis, that is, of the predictability ensured by the
natural and organic order. Therefore, the course of the crisis
traces a 'revolution' – in both the common and the astronomical sense of the term: a 'return' to order or order as 'return'.
Because it was so strictly inscribed in the cosmic order, the physicians of antiquity could diagnose and prognosticate crisis at
the same time. It would be modernity that, while retaining the
strict connection between crisis and revolution, would overturn
the meaning of this relation.

---

15   Suffice to consider that Galen dedicated an entire treatise to this topic,
De Diebus Decretoriis.

16   Hippocrates, 'Epidemics I', p. 185.

II. MODERN AGE

Nowhere does it come to have an effect but always only 'criticism'; and criticism itself again has no effect but only comes to see further criticism.
Friedrich Nietzsche, *On the Advantage and Disadvantage of History for Life*

4

Before the Revolution

The term crisis was only absorbed into the economic lexicon in the nineteenth century, despite it being one of the fields in which the concept appears most frequently today. Its first occurrence in economics was in 1772, in reference to the financial crisis of that year.[1] However, this was an isolated case, and its use remained sporadic in the following decades. It was only during the nineteenth century that the term 'crisis' was more commonly related to the economy. The premises of that economic mode of government that today characterizes neoliberal hegemony can be traced to that epoch.

It cannot be a mere coincidence that — as proof of a matrix that persists over time — the use in economics of the word 'crisis' recalls the medical meaning the term had when it first appeared

---

1   The word 'crisis' appears in the subtitle of James Boswell's 1772 pamphlet *Reflections on the Late Alarming Bankruptcies in Scotland. Addressed to All Ranks. But Particularly to the Different Classes of Men from Whom Payments May Soon Be Demanded. With Advice to Such, How to Conduct Themselves at This Crisis*.

in the Greek world: 'disease', 'imbalance', 'diagnosis', and at the same time 'prognosis'. As Koselleck points out:

> From the 1840s on, the economically based concept of crisis permeates the growing literature of social criticisms ... 'Crisis' was well suited to conceptualize both the emergencies resulting from contemporary constitutional or class specific upheavals, as well as the distress caused by industry, technology, and the capitalist market economy. These could be treated as symptoms of a serious disease or as a disturbance of the economy's equilibrium.[2]

This medical meaning of the term 'crisis' prevailed until the eighteenth century. Foucault unwittingly confirms this in his analysis of the epidemics that swept through Europe in the seventeenth and eighteenth centuries. Despite finding it unusual that the word was used in the medical lexicon, his definition of crisis comes from the tradition of ancient medicine: 'This phenomenon of sudden bolting, which regularly occurs and is also regularly nullified, can be called, roughly – not exactly in medical terminology, since the word was already used to designate something else – the crisis. The crisis is this phenomenon of sudden, circular bolting that can only be checked either by a higher, natural mechanism, or by an artificial mechanism.'[3] Suffice it to say that, even in 1754, in Diderot and D'Alembert's *Encyclopédie*, under the entry 'Crise' by Théophile De Bordeu, 'crisis' appears only as a medical word, which – according to the definition proposed by Galen on the basis of the teaching of Hippocrates' school – draws on the forensic meaning of

---

2   Koselleck, 'Crisis', p. 391.
3   Foucault, *Security, Territory, Population*, p. 61.

judgment. Basing his entry heavily on Galen's theory of crisis, De Bordeu understands the judgment as concerning the course of an illness, which becomes 'critical' when it reaches the stage of struggle, of the conflict between life and death:

> Galen tells us that the word *crisis* is a forensic term that physicians have adopted and which means, strictly speaking, *judgment.* Hippocrates calls *crisis* every change that leads to a disease. He also states that there is a *crisis* in a disease when it gets serious or improves considerably, when it degenerates into another disease or ceases altogether. Galen claims, almost in the same sense, that the *crisis* is a sudden change of the disease for better or for worse; this has meant that several authors have considered the crisis as a sort of struggle between nature and disease; a struggle in which nature can win or perish: they have also argued that death can sometimes be considered as the crisis of a disease.[4]

The definition of 'crisis' that De Bordeu takes from ancient medicine is that the crisis is not the time of the diagnosis of healing, but rather the 'most acute' moment of the disease, when the outcome is the most uncertain and the physician's judgment can be 'decisive'. This definition is more in tune with the discourse of modernity that was starting to take shape at the time.

Around the same time as Diderot and D'Alembert's *Encyclopédie* was published, an equivalent encyclopaedia appeared in Germany: the *Grosses vollständiges Universal-Lexicon* by Johann

---

4   T. De Bordeu, 'Crise' [1754], in D. Diderot and D'Alembert, *Encyclopédie, ou Dictionnaire raisonné des sciences, des arts et des métiers*, Stuttgart, 1966, p. 471 (translation by SP). De Bordeu was an important member of the 'vitalist' School of Medicine of Montpelier.

Heinrich Zedler. It also contains an entry for 'crisis', and also accounts for the medical meaning only.[5] But there is one differ-ence from the French entry that is relevant for our discussion. While in De Bordeu's definition the meaning of crisis is basi-cally derived from Galen's doctrine, and therefore the word indicates the moment in which the course of an illness suddenly takes a sharp turn for the better or for the worse, for Zedler, it is the re-establishment of the initial health that prevails, or better: 'the crisis acquires its meaning as a result of a judgment'.[6] The crisis is therefore the healthy outcome following a judgment rather than the opportune moment for the decision.

Furthermore, Zedler maintains that ancient physicians – beginning with Hippocrates and Galen – gave the term 'crisis' many meanings. But the 'confusion' that ensued was solved in his own time: 'Nowadays it is called crisis that salutary influence of nature through which the material of the disease is expelled from the body, which is then released from its perishing and from disease.'[7] In short, crisis now indicates simply recovery from illness, the positive outcome of 'secreting' the disease from the body. At this point, Zedler distinguishes between a 'crisis imperfecta', when nature moves the cause of the disease from the most noble to the less noble parts of the body without

---

5   The same can be said also of the dictionaries in English. *The Oxford English Dictionary* attests that the first and oldest meaning of 'crisis' is medical (sixteenth century), while during the seventeenth century – the century of revolutions in England – the medical sense of crisis entered the political field. The oldest political use the OED reports dates back to 1627, when Sir B. Rudyard stated: 'this is the Chrysis of Parliaments; we shall know by this if Parliaments live or die'. *The Oxford English Dictionary*, Vol. IV, Oxford: Clarendon Press, 1989, p. 27.

6   J.H. Zedler, *Grosses vollständiges Universal-Lexicon*, Halle-Leipzig 1733, p. 1652 (translation by SP).

7   Ibid.

expelling it altogether, and a 'crisis perfecta', 'when through natural movements the whole cause of the disease is expelled and therefore the body suddenly returns to the previous healthy condition'.[8] In this definition of crisis, it seems clear that the shift in meaning from the moment of judgment and decision to the outcome of the judgment ascribes crisis to the *natural* government – or self-government – of the body. The judgment at issue here is only the diagnosis of nature's spontaneous course towards recovery, since the body is naturally oriented towards the preservation of life: a 'perfect crisis' is thus complete recovery. If there is no complete recovery, then either the crisis is imperfect or there is no crisis at all (and so there is death). Zedler solves the 'confusion' that he sees in ancient medicine's conception of crisis by restoring the notion of crisis given by Hippocrates, thereby dismissing the modern definition inherited from Galen. As I will argue, in much more recent times, Zedler's 'naturalistic' connotation of crisis, which reduces the dynamics of the forced decision to the extreme consequence of the lack of alternatives, has found application outside the medical field.

However, the medical origin of crisis inherited by modernity and absorbed into the political discourse is not that of Zedler, but rather that given by De Bordeu in the *Encyclopédie*, in line with Galen. As a result, *conflict* acquired a fundamental role in the *dispositif* that took shape in modernity. Within the *dispositif* of crisis, *conflict* is a symptom of the 'disease' that has infected the order, yet, at the same time, it also represents the first stage of a possible recovery, since, in the critical condition, it entails the discernment of and distinction between a healing path and a fatal path. Hence, conflict is the condition of the

8   Ibid., p. 1653.

possible 'decision', which – and this is key – cannot but be directed towards health, towards the preservation of life. The exit from the crisis – i.e. its solution – can only be a restoration of the order prior to the disease: health and life. It is through this semantic spectrum that the *concept* of crisis enters modernity, already implying a certain idea of conflict. Koselleck writes that the 'use of the concept of crisis is meant to reduce the room for manoeuvre, forcing the actors to choose between diametrically opposed alternatives'.[9] The concept of crisis may offer the clearest alternative: that between life and death. If the 'normal' condition is health, which crisis and disease jeopardize, to decide in favour of life means to choose the pre-existing order.

However, the transition to modernity of the *dispositif* of crisis resulted in the loss of its fundamental sense of being the forced decision towards the preservation of the life and order prior to the disease – the meaning that crisis had in antiquity – and its replacement with the prevalence of the moment of the 'decision'. If choice is expressed in relation to an alternative that is in some ways already predetermined, decision does not necessarily presuppose an alternative: it can open up a field of possibility which up until that moment was unforeseen.[10] Revolutionary politics liberates the decision from the model of a

---

9   Koselleck, 'Crisis', p. 370.

10   As we will see, with the demise of modernity and its paradigms (including that of the decision), neoliberalism employs Rational Choice Theory, reducing the decision to a choice. However, Jon Elster, a key theorist of Rational Choice Theory, clearly distinguishes between choice and decision: 'Although all choices are decisions, the converse is not true. When I decide to pick up the book I have been reading, I need not have any explicit alternative in mind ... No choice is involved.' J. Elster, *Explaining Social Behavior: More Nuts and Bolts for the Social Sciences*, Cambridge: Cambridge University Press, 2015, p. 187.

choice between alternatives, introducing decision into the use of crisis. Modernity, therefore, brings the possibility of the new into the notion of crisis, which became part of the orientation towards the future typical of the 'revolution'. The modern idea of revolution – as disruption, discontinuity, and projection into the future – converted the function of the *dispositif* of the crisis so that it gradually lost its medical connotations, leading to the term being used in other and varied contexts. It is important to reflect for a moment on this transition.

At the dawn of modernity, Niccolò Machiavelli was already contemplating the possibility that the 'return to health' of the political body could also be considered a 'renewal' induced by an 'alteration', a 'crisis':

> It is a very true thing that all worldly things have a limit to their life; but generally those go the whole course that is ordered for them by heaven, that do not disorder their body but keep it ordered so that either it does not alter or, if it alters, it is for its safety and not to its harm. Because I am speaking of mixed bodies, such as republics and sects, I say that those alterations are for safety that lead them back towards their beginnings. So those are better ordered and have longer life that by means of their orders can often be renewed or indeed that through some accident outside the said order come to the said renewal. And it is a thing clearer than light that these bodies do not last if they do not renew themselves.[11]

It was, however, with the Enlightenment that this inversion of the orientation of revolution was put to test historically,

---

11 N. Machiavelli, *Discourses on Livy*, Chicago: University of Chicago Press, 1996, p. 209 [III, 1].

showing that the choice in favour of life did not have to be a conservative one. Indeed, in *The Social Contract* (1762), Jean-Jacques Rousseau not only connects crisis and revolution, but, while still adopting the medical metaphor of crisis, also suggests that the return of the body politic – of the 'people' – to health can occur through the 'disruption' and 'upheavals' of possible violent transformations and changes. Of course, Rousseau sees these cases as rare exceptions, and remains convinced that the memory of the past should be a discouragement from considering that changing the current conditions – even when they are already hopelessly compromised – is useful or healthy, but he does not rule out that change can restore health and full recovery in sick and corrupt peoples:

Peoples, like men, are amenable only when they are young; in old age they become incorrigible. Once customs are established and prejudices ingrained, it is a dangerous and futile enterprise to try to reform them; the people cannot bear to have the disease treated, even in order to destroy it, like those stupid and fearful patients who tremble at the sight of the physician. Nonetheless, just as some illnesses shake up men's minds and deprive them of the memory of the past, sometimes there are periods of violence during the lifetimes of states, when revolutions have the same effect on nations as certain medical crises on individuals, and revulsion against the past acts like a loss of memory; the state is then, in the flames of civil war, reborn from its ashes, so to speak, and, escaping from the embrace of death, recovers its youthful strength.[12]

---

12   J.-J. Rousseau, *The Social Contract*, Oxford: Oxford University Press, 1999, p. 80 [II/8].

Although, like in antiquity, for Rousseau too, crisis properly concerns individuals and can only refer to the body politic by analogy, it is clear from this passage – which is very much in line with his overall thought – that the healthy condition is always an original condition to which we must return. In very rare circumstances revolutions can bring about such a 'return', to restore and 'revive' a sick body, but they never generate new life. This demonstrates the persistence and the force that the Greek *dispositif* of *krisis* still retained: 'But such events are rare and exceptional, and the reason for the exception always lies in the way in which a particular state is constituted … Civil strife can then destroy it [one nation], but a revolution cannot revive it; as soon as its chains are broken, it falls into fragments and no longer exists.'[13] However, in Rousseau, perhaps for the first time, crisis begins from and operates within a condition of sickness rather than health – thus not on a body that gets ill but on one that is already ill. The preservation of this condition of illness would lead to death: health remains the aim to be pursued through the return to the original state, but it cannot be achieved through the conservation of the current order.

Yet, as Koselleck reminds us in *Critique and Crisis*, Rousseau's use of the notion of crisis remained fairly isolated at the time. Although it resulted in the French Revolution, the eighteenth century was, in fact, the century of criticism rather than crisis: 'Given the prevailing view of the State as a body, it was not far-fetched to apply the medical term "crisis" to the political arena. But Rousseau was the first to apply the term to the body politic, the "corps politique".'[14] For Rousseau's

<hr />

13   Ibid.
14   R. Koselleck, *Critique and Crisis: Enlightenment and Pathogenesis of Modern Society*, Cambridge, MA: MIT Press, 1988, p. 167.

contemporaries, Enlightenment thinkers included, the medical
and organic origin of crisis did not involve or imply that division and dualism from which it would be possible to carry out
a judgment for or against. In short, it was perhaps clearer then
than it is today that crisis did not require a position external to
the dominant power from which the judgment and the decision
could follow; rather, the judgment of the crisis is always internal to the dynamics of the crisis itself and it tends – as pointed
out above – to endorse and validate rather than to oppose.
Thus, it is not surprising that, with the exception of Rousseau
and a few others,[15] in the eighteenth century the term 'crisis'
was very rarely used in politics. Instead, the term 'criticism'
prevailed: 'The term "crisis" on the other hand was rarely used
in the eighteenth century and certainly cannot be considered
a central concept. This fact is not a statistical fortuity; rather
there is a specific connection between it and the ascendancy of
criticism.'[16] The two terms can be assimilated to one another
only superficially. Both derive from the same judicial root,
yet, while 'crisis' immediately entered the medical lexicon and
became stable, from ancient times to the Middle Ages 'criticism' and 'critic' inscribed themselves in a different genealogy
and therefore retained the connotation of the 'ability to judge',
but only in the fields of philology, biblical exegesis, logic and
aesthetics.[17]

---

15   'The term [crisis] is found not in the work of the progressives but
in the writings of philosophers committed to the cyclic view of history: in
Rousseau … and in Rousseau's amicable opponent Diderot.' Ibid., pp. 161–2.

16   Ibid., p. 102.

17   See K. Röttgers, 'Kritik', in O. Brunner, W. Conze, and R. Koselleck
(eds.), Geschichtliche Grundbegriffe. Historisches Lexikon zur politisch-sozialen
Sprache in Deutschland, Vol. 3, Stuttgart: Klett-Cotta, 2004, pp. 651–75.

It was criticism and not crisis that laid the ground for the French Revolution. In Koselleck's view, however, Enlightenment thinkers tended 'hypocritically' to hide the political scope of their so-called 'moral' criticism, which claims to be such only because it proceeds from outside the state and politics:

> To that extent the concept of crisis encompasses a spectrum of events, with no room for dualistic dichotomies that do not touch on areas outside the State. However, crisis in the Rousseauesque sense of political anarchy, crisis as the end of order, the collapse of all property relations, convulsion and unpredictable unrest; crisis as the political crisis of the State as a whole, was not the central meaning which bourgeois crisis-consciousness attached to it. Rather, pre-revolutionary crisis-consciousness fed on the type of political criticism practised by the bourgeoisie within the Absolutist State.[18]

Criticism produces a space that is autonomous from the dominant power and makes it possible to judge and question power itself. The political concept of crisis as 'final decision' derives from Enlightenment criticism and not vice versa. This criticism moves from the 'external' position of the bourgeoisie to the dominant power, and can distinguish and separate from the body politic a political part which is a potential alternative. Koselleck is very clear about this: 'Once the State becomes involved in the critical process, its "pour et contre" turns into the either/or of a crisis that inevitably forces the political decision.'[19] The 'decisive crisis' is the political product of criticism and, we might add, characterized modernity's idea of crisis.

---

18 Koselleck, *Critique and Crisis*, p. 168.
19 Ibid., p. 172.

This modern concept of crisis – the concept of crisis that is the object of Koselleck's analysis, of which we have given an account above – ended up almost entirely losing its previous medical and biological characteristics. Perhaps this is why Koselleck writes that the concept of crisis today 'has been transformed to fit the uncertainties of whatever might be favored at a given moment'. One could also argue that the 'modern concept' of crisis has lost its hold on reality, on society and contemporary politics. Indeed, like Carl Schmitt – whom he mentions several times in *Critique and Crisis* and credits as a key interlocutor – Koselleck does not attach political significance to crisis, except when it leads to a 'decision', and finds a 'solution' in the reality and concreteness of the decision. In Koselleck's discourse, criticism and crisis seem to share the semantic spectrum of the Greek verb *krinein*: criticism 'judges' and crisis 'decides' in the political sense. In his 1985 text on crisis, Koselleck is even more explicit in defining the semantic model of crisis as that consisting in the 'final decision'. He recovers the figure of *katechon* in Schmitt's political theology, as an 'answer' to the decline of modern politics following the inability of crisis to provide the 'final decision'. While the theological model of the final decision was the Last Judgment, the political decision no longer puts an end to the cycles of crises, but, in keeping with the theological meaning and function of *katechon*, 'delays' or 'withholds' the end, the establishment of which is no longer the prerogative of the political decision as it was in the modern paradigm of crisis: 'So, the question can be raised as to whether our semantic model of crisis as final decision has gained more chances of realization than it has ever had before. If this is the case, everything would depend upon directing all our powers toward deterring destruction. The cat-echon is also a theological answer to crisis.'[20]

When crisis no longer provides the condition for the 'final decision', the function of criticism as judgment also changes. Being a judgment without decision, political criticism is inef-fective and risks becoming a mere exercise – increasingly more widespread and increasingly less influential – that falls within the remit of the administration of crisis as an art of government. Friedrich Nietzsche had already identified this degeneration of modern criticism in *On the Advantage and Disadvantage of History for Life* (1874): 'Their critical pen ... never ceases to flow for they [our critics] have lost control over it and are directed by it, instead of directing it.'[21]

20   R. Koselleck, 'Some Questions Regarding the Conceptual History of "Crisis"' [1985], in *The Practice of Conceptual History: Timing History, Spacing Concepts*, Stanford: Stanford University Press, 2002, p. 247.
21   F. Nietzsche, *On the Advantage and Disadvantage of History for Life*, Indianapolis: Hackett, 1980, p. 32.

5
New Life: Marx's Use of Crisis

Although still adopting the medical connotation of crisis, Rousseau changed the condition in which crisis comes into being (not health, but disease), thereby triggering a substantial adjustment in its use. But in order for crisis to assume a fully 'political' meaning in modernity – thus marking a rupture from the exclusively medical and judicial use of the Greek *krisis* – the term borrowed from criticism the sense of the 'final decision' it had had in the Enlightenment court, and from the French Revolution the idea of a 'new life' that breaks the cyclical return to the original state of health as the only possibility of salvation from disease. Written just before the French Revolution, Kant's Preface to the *Critique of Pure Reason* (1781) no longer excluded religion and state from the judgment of the tribunal of reason.[1]

---

1 'Our age is, in especial degree, the age of criticism, and to criticism everything must submit. Religion through its sanctity and law-giving through its majesty may seek to exempt themselves from it. But they then awaken just suspicion, and cannot claim the sincere respect which reason accords only to that which has been able to sustain the test of free and open examination.' I. Kant, *Critique of Pure Reason*, London: Palgrave Macmillan, 2007, pp. 4–5, note 1.

The Revolution historically pronounced this judgment. Saint-Simon, for instance, envisions crisis as 'regenerative disease' and the engine of progress: 'Revolutions are atrocious diseases, and at the same time inevitable diseases. The great progresses of the human spirit are the results of great crises, and these progresses prepare new crises.'[2]

While in modern political discourse, crisis appears as the 'final decision' and the possibility of the 'new', in economic discourse, crisis is introduced into the lexicon with the medical connotation that orients its *dispositif* towards self-preservation – thus remaining closer to its ancient meaning. Generally speaking, economic crises clearly reveal the imbalance and difference between a state of health and a state of sickness in the capitalist market system, and therefore very clearly indicate their own solution. The assumption is that safeguarding and strengthening the state of health means ensuring the survival and existence of both the system and order. Karl Marx was the first to try to introduce those 'political' qualities that marked the passage of crisis through modernity and its revolutions into economic discourse – in the *dispositif* of the economic crisis. Among these political qualities was the possibility of the 'new', of a political alternative that actually presented itself as such. Such an alternative could be produced through the practice of criticism. For the young Marx, criticism's 'participation in politics' and political outcome were already a given: 'nothing prevents us from making criticism of politics, participation in politics, and therefore *real* struggles, the starting point of our criticism, and from

---

2   H. Saint-Simon, *Introduction aux travaux scientifiques du XIXe siècle* [1807–8], in Œuvres, Vol. VI, Paris: Editions Anthropos, 1966, p. 166 (translation by SP).

identifying our criticism with them'.[3] We could argue that the young Marx's political critique made explicit what was implicit in Enlightenment critique – 'the crisis ... lies hidden in the criticism'[4] – thus making the political decision proceed directly from criticism's judgment. In this way, criticism becomes the bearer of a political alternative. A few years later, Marx would propose a critique of the capitalist use of crisis. It was criticism that allowed him to conceive of an alternative political use of the *dispositif* of the economic crisis, whose function, nature, and medical origin remained the same.

In *The Communist Manifesto* (1848), Marx and Engels use the term 'epidemic' to describe the virulence of economic crises, which destroy not only goods, but also and above all the productive forces that capitalist relations generate in industrial production. These crises – in particular, commercial crises – end up involving the entire society and therefore the 'population'. Hence the social and political domination of the bourgeoisie is threatened: 'In these crises there breaks out an epidemic that, in all earlier epochs, would have seemed an absurdity – the epidemic of over-production. Society suddenly finds itself put back into a state of momentary barbarism; it appears as if a famine, a universal war of devastation had cut off the supply

---

3   K. Marx, Letter to Ruge (September 1843), in *The Collected Works of Karl Marx and Frederick Engels*, Vol. 3, New York: International Publishers, 1975, p. 144. In the same letter to Arnold Ruge: 'we do not dogmatically anticipate the world, but only want to find the new world through criticism of the old one ... [I]f constructing the future and settling everything for all times are not our affair, it is all the more clear what we have to accomplish at present: I am referring to *ruthless criticism* of all that exists, ruthless both in the sense of not being afraid of the results it arrives at and in the sense of being just as little afraid of conflict with the powers that be.' Ibid., p. 142.

4   Koselleck, *Critique and Crisis*, p. 103.

of every means of subsistence.'[5] As we have seen, Foucault showed how the term 'crisis' was used to describe the epidemics of the seventeenth and eighteenth centuries. We have to return to this period – with its epidemics and famines – to see how medical and economic knowledge were radically transformed and became interwoven as a result of the crisis. In the wake of the crisis, this change in medical knowledge led to the setting up of public health institutions, while for economic knowledge the mercantile system started to take precedence over the physiocratic doctrine. Since, to this day, we still describe the spread of an economic crisis in terms of 'contagion', it should be no surprise that Marx and Engels compare capitalist crises to epidemics. This epidemic aspect is therefore a constant and peculiar feature of capitalist economy, whose expansion and degeneration help re-establish and strengthen the bourgeois relationship of domination. Marx and Engels see the *dispositif* of the crisis adopted by the capitalist-bourgeois system as a function of government, that is, as a rebalancing of the dispro-portion between the dominant relations of production and the productive forces that exceed them:

> The conditions of bourgeois society are too narrow to comprise the wealth created by them. And how does the bourgeoisie get over these crises? On the one hand by enforced destruction of a mass of productive forces; on the other, by the conquest of new markets, and by the more thorough exploitation of the old ones. That is to say, by paving the way for more extensive and more destructive crises, and by diminishing the means whereby crises are prevented.[6]

5   K. Marx and F. Engels, *The Communist Manifesto*, London: Penguin, 2002, p. 226.
6   Ibid.

Although I will not go into much detail here, it is important to remember that Marx and Engels theorized the cyclical nature of capitalist crises and the vital role they play in the system's restructuring process. In the *Communist Manifesto*, Marx and Engels still adopt the bourgeois conception of economic crises, so-called 'cycle theory'. In this theory, crises indicate the imbalances of the capitalist economic system, to which the system responds by re-establishing a balance, that is, the natural regularity of the cycle. Crises are diseases that disturb the health of the system, the condition of normality that must be returned to. And, as Marx and Engels argue, crises are also functional to the restructuring and strengthening of the system, which preserves itself 'by paving the way for more extensive and more destructive crises' and, at the same time, expands – like an epidemic – up to the limits of the world market. For Marx and Engels, economic crises appear as anything but accidental and contingent; being instead structural to the system, they remain immanent to the economic cycle. They are the way in which the bourgeois political order is preserved, reacting to the disease and returning it to health. In short, crises are the prerogative of the bourgeois art of government.

In *The Eighteenth Brumaire of Louis Bonaparte* of 1852, a few years after the publication of the *Manifesto*, Marx also finds in 'revolutionary crises' the bourgeois tendency towards the cyclical repetition of history, towards a return to the past as a means to legitimize and endorse the transformation of the present. But while economic crisis helps to re-establish, if not to reinvigorate, the given order – which is the beneficial effect of its 'revolution' – a political 'revolutionary crisis' turns into a farce if it seeks in the repetition of the past a historical legitimation for the transformation of the present:

Hegel remarks somewhere that all facts and personages of great importance in world history occur, as it were, twice. He forgot to add: the first time as tragedy, the second as farce. Men make their own history, but they do not make it just as they please; they do not make it under circumstances chosen by themselves, but under circumstances directly encountered, given and transmitted from the past. The tradition of all the dead generations weighs like a nightmare on the brain of the living. And just when they seem engaged in revolutionising themselves and things, in creating something that has never yet existed, precisely in such periods of revolutionary crisis they anxiously conjure up the spirits of the past to their service and borrow from them names, battle-cries and costumes in order to present the new scene of world history in this time-honoured disguise and this borrowed language.[7]

A proletarian revolution can only occur if it takes a different path from bourgeois revolutions. The storm of the *Sturm und Drang* of the eighteenth-century bourgeois revolution was followed not by the overthrowing of the order, but rather by the 'crapulent depression' and nausea (*Katzenjammer*) that follows drunkenness or disease. The social body is not born again as a new life, but comes out weakened and exposed to other diseases that will soon strike:

> Bourgeois revolutions, like those of the eighteenth century, storm swiftly from success to success, their dramatic effects outdo each other, men and things seem set in sparkling brilliants, ecstasy is the

---

7   K. Marx, *The Eighteenth Brumaire of Louis Bonaparte*, in *The Collected Works of Karl Marx and Frederick Engels*, Vôl. 11, New York: International Publishers, 1975, pp. 103–4.

everyday spirit, but they are short-lived, soon they have attained their zenith, and a long crapulent depression (*Katzenjammer*) seizes society before it learns soberly to assimilate the results of its storm-and-stress period (*Drang- und Sturmperiode*).[8]

A successful proletarian revolution must first of all stop the cyclical repetition of history, turn away from the duplication of the past and point to the future:

> proletarian revolutions, like those of the nineteenth century, criticise themselves constantly, interrupt themselves continually in their own course, come back to the apparently accomplished in order to begin it afresh, deride with unmerciful thoroughness the inadequacies, weaknesses and paltrinesses of their first attempts, seem to throw down their adversary only in order that he may draw new strength from the earth and rise again, more gigantic, before them, and recoil again and again from the indefinite prodigiousness of their own aims, until a situation has been created which makes all turning back impossible.[9]

A few years later, Marx understood that, in order for a real proletarian revolution to break out historically, it was necessary to work at the economic level, where class power and class exploitation is built and structured; it was therefore necessary to operate with the *dispositifs* of the capitalist economy, converting their use. Moving beyond the *Manifesto*, which described only the bourgeois use of the crisis, Marx now developed a theory of economic crises that attempted to adapt this *dispositif*

---

8   Ibid., p. 106.
9   Ibid., pp. 106–7.

in a revolutionary sense, towards a proletarian use of the crisis. Believing that the economic crisis of 1857 would be 'final', thus fatal for capital, Marx developed an alternative conception of crisis in the *Grundrisse* that was not functional to the cyclical restructuring of the system but brought with it the opportunity to overthrow it. Marx takes the bourgeoisie's previous exclusive use of the *dispositif* of crisis and deploys it against them: he takes the crisis from within the capitalist economic cycle and makes it an independent moment – the moment of the irreparable rupture of the cycle.

Thus, the discourse shifts from the historical-political to the economic plane, and the lexicon of crisis assumes medical connotations. In this way, Marx absorbed the *dispositif* of the crisis that was already active in capitalism but reversed its terms: seeming to follow the steps of Rousseau's discourse, the state of health of the capitalist system was now compromised, the disease had become the 'norm'. Capitalism was sick, and its course led inexorably – according to internal necessity – towards its extinction, as indicated by the theory of the *tendency of the rate of profit to fall*. Thus, recovery from illness no longer meant the restoration of and return to an old equilibrium, but moving towards a 'new' order, a 'new' and different state of health. Thus, Marx bent the *dispositif* of crisis towards the creation of 'something that has never yet existed'. The revolution no longer looks backwards. Contemplating the new as an intrinsic part of crisis, Marx applies the configuration of the political crisis to the economic crisis. And yet, this something 'new', the proletariat, would be able to overthrow the system and regenerate society – creating a new order – precisely because it was born *within* the system of capitalist production. Etymologically, the word *proletariat* alludes to the ability to 'generate life', to the possibility of 'reproduction'.

The medical lexicon Marx uses is much more than just a legacy of the original root of crisis. This passage from the *Grundrisse* almost sounds like a medical prognosis:

> The growing incompatibility between the productive development of society and its hitherto existing relations of production expresses itself in bitter contradictions, crises, and spasms. The violent destruction of capital not by relations external to it, but rather as a condition of its self-preservation, is the most striking form in which advice is given it to be gone and to give room to a higher state of social production.[10]

It is not only the terms used that suggest a medical interpretation of this passage, but also the course of the crisis it describes: it is capitalism's 'self-preservation' that leads to its extinction, following an evolution entirely 'internal' to its organism. It is as if capitalism would inevitably be brought to an end by an autoimmune disease.[11] In short, the Marxian notion of crisis and the notion used by capitalism share the same *lack of an alternative*: the application is different, but the *dispositif* is the same. Of course, in Marx, the necessary character of the *dispositif* of crisis is translated in a political sense, to the advantage of the proletarian revolution.

---

10   K. Marx, *Grundrisse*, New York: Vintage, 1973, pp. 749–50.

11   On the biopolitical meaning of this 'immunity' *dispositif*, see R. Esposito, *Immunitas: The Protection and Negation of Life*, Cambridge: Polity, 2011.

6

Crisis as Interregnum: Gramsci

Antonio Gramsci retains the Marxian interpretation of the *dispositif* of crisis but seems also to revive the connotation of the Greek *krisis* as 'preservation of the order'. As with the epidemics, there is a 'mortal danger' that threatens the social body. Adapting the Aristotelian approach of the 'government of crisis', Gramsci attributes the 'use of crisis' to the rulers: although it is not their immediate prerogative, its use is mostly under their authority. Gramsci explicitly defines as 'organic' a crisis which is governed by the leading class without calling into question its hegemony. In fact, crisis ends up representing the opportunity, in the presence of a 'mortal danger', to bring the social body 'under the banner of a single party' – which I will call the 'party of life':

The crisis creates situations which are dangerous in the short run, since the various strata of the population are not all capable of orienting themselves equally swiftly, or of reorganizing with the same rhythm. The traditional ruling class, which has numerous trained cadres, changes men and programmes and, with greater speed than is achieved by the subordinate classes, reabsorbs the control that was slipping from its grasp. Perhaps it may make sacrifices, and expose itself to an uncertain future by demagogic promises; but it retains power, reinforces it for the time being, and uses it to crush its adversary and disperse his leading cadres ... The passage of the troops of many different parties under the banner of a single party, which better represents and resumes the needs of the entire class, is an organic and normal phenomenon ... It represents the fusion of an entire social class under a single leadership, which alone is held to be capable of solving an overriding problem of its existence and of fending off a mortal danger.[1]

'Organic' crisis might correspond to what Zedler, referring to ancient physicians, called a 'perfect crisis', since the leading classes and rulers restore and strengthen their own hegemony *from within* the order. However, Gramsci also envisions another use of crisis, which corresponds to what Zedler called an 'imperfect crisis', due to its not being organic: the 'mortal danger' is governed and order is restored *from the outside*, with the appearance on the scene of the charismatic leader: 'When the crisis does not find this organic solution, but that of the charismatic leader, it means that a static equilibrium exists ...; it means that no group, neither the conservatives nor the progressives, has the strength for victory, and that even the conservative group needs a master.'[2] Gramsci mentions Marx's *The Eighteenth Brumaire of Louis Bonaparte* and the rise of Louis Bonaparte as a

---

1   A. Gramsci, *Selections from the Prison Notebooks*, ed. Q. Hoare and G. Nowell Smith, London: Lawrence & Wishart, 1971, pp. 210–11 [Q 4, 69].
2   Ibid.

'non-organic' result of the 'organic' counterrevolution carried out by the bourgeois 'party of order' after 1848. He deploys the notion of a non-organic crisis also to explain the rise of fascism in Italy. Fascism – along with today's forms of populism, to which I will return later – is the heir of 'Bonapartism', which appears on the political scene when the impasse in the class struggle allows the emergence of the 'unorganized mass' of the people, which goes beyond the divisions between classes.[3] In this non-organic solution to the crisis, there is a direct relationship between the charismatic leader and the mass that does not depend on the power relations between classes that rule over the organic crisis.

It might be thought that Gramsci's organic crisis corresponds to Marx's idea of the bourgeois use of the capitalist crisis. However, for Gramsci, the crisis in the ruling class's hegemony does not necessarily imply the possibility of an alternative use of crisis, or express the symptom of a new social life that arises from within to assert itself as a cure for the disease. As in Marx, so for Gramsci, crisis reverses the usual relationship between life and death, health and disease, thus configuring *a suspension between an impending death and a new life that is not yet born.* However – and this is his fundamental difference with Marx – Gramsci holds that it is not entirely from 'within' the crisis that the possibility of a new life is produced: 'The crisis consists precisely in the fact that the old is dying and the new cannot be born; in this interregnum a great variety of morbid symptoms appear.'[4] In the interregnum, the perpetuation of the old delays

3   See Marx, *The Eighteenth Brumaire of Louis Bonaparte*, p. 121. The English edition translates 'unorganische Masse' (non-organic mass) with 'unorganized masses'.

4   Gramsci, *Selections from the Prison Notebooks*, p. 276 [Q 3, 34].

the advent of the new, which, as Gramsci says, cannot be born in this context of crisis. In fact, not only does the crisis not aid the affirmation of the new, it restrains and withholds it.

In my terms, the function of crisis is defined according to the use of its *dispositif*. Gramsci had in mind both the political crisis that led to the establishment of fascism in Italy and the economic crisis of 1929. He identifies in the so-called 'passive revolution' a transformation oriented to conservation, which represents the point of contact between political crisis and economic crisis, which end up coinciding with one another.[5] With a 'crisis of political authority', the 'ruling classes' lose the consent of the masses and must become 'dominant' to retain power. In this situation, the government acts on a more immediately economic level and the politics that results is the 'cynical' politics of crisis as art of government: 'The death of the old ideologies takes the form of scepticism with regard to all theories and general formulae; of application to the pure economic fact (earnings, etc.), and to a form of politics which is not simply realistic in fact (this is always the case) but which is cynical in its immediate manifestation.'[6] Gramsci considered the interregnum as a

---

5 Thus, Gramsci analysed the bond between economy and politics that the passive revolution of his time produced: 'Passive revolution would be brought about through the fact of transforming the economic structure in a "reformist" fashion from an individualistic to a planned economy (a command economy). The creation of an economy "mid-way" between one of the pure individualist type and one that, in the full sense, functions according to a plan would allow the passage to more advanced political and cultural forms without radical and destructive cataclysms of an exterminatory kind.' A. Gramsci, *Further Selections from the Prison Notebooks*, ed. D. Boothman, London: Lawrence & Wishart, 1995, p. 418 [Q 8, 236]. On 'passive revolution' and 'organic crisis' and their relationship, see P.D. Thomas, *The Gramscian Moment: Philosophy, Hegemony and Marxism*, Leiden: Brill, 2009.

6 Gramsci, *Further Selections from the Prison Notebooks*, p. 276 [Q 4, 69].

condition with uncertain outcomes, with no necessary or automatic way out in favour of the subordinate classes: 'Will the interregnum, the crisis whose historically normal solution is blocked in this way, necessarily be resolved in favour of a restoration of the old? Given the character of the ideologies, that can be ruled out – yet not in an absolute sense.'[7] He wrote this in the early 1930s. We all know what happened next.

If we recover and radicalize the Gramscian notion of 'interregnum',[8] we have a form of government that contemplates coercion and the indefinite duration of the crisis. In Gramsci's terms, crisis takes the form of a *dispositif*: it is 'a complex process, as in many other phenomena, and not a unique "fact" repeated in various forms through a cause having one single origin'.[9] Since we are 'dealing with a process and not an event',[10] crisis does not lead inexorably to an end – salvation or death – for the suspension between life and death can last indefinitely. Therefore, the interregnum does not simply define a period of transition, but a particular art of government that the capitalist use of the *dispositif* configures;[11] an art of government that

---

7   Ibid.

8   Gramsci's notion of interregnum has recently been recovered to interpret the current situation, especially with regard to the Greek crisis of 2015. See Z. Bauman and C. Bordoni, *State of Crisis*, Cambridge: Polity, 2014; É. Balibar, 'The Relations Greece and Europa Need', Verso Blog, 12 May 2015; B. Caccia and S. Mezzadra, 'Under the Sky of "Interregnum"', EuroNomade, 15 September 2015.

9   Gramsci, *Further Selections from the Prison Notebooks*, pp. 351–2 [Q 15, § 5].

10   Ibid., p. 352 [Q 15, § 5].

11   Wolfgang Streeck also uses Gramsci's notion of 'interregnum' to define the current stage of capitalism, which is slowly but steadily declining as a result of entropy. According to Streeck, capitalism's interregnum – its agony – will last until neoliberalism, which invests in individuals, reveals its unsustainability without new social bonds and new forms of commonality. See

acts by postponing the equilibrium resulting from the treatment or alleged treatment of the disease. Diseases continue to appear one after the other:

> the development of capitalism has been a 'continual crisis', if one can say that, i.e. an extremely rapid movement of elements that mutually balanced and immunized one another. At a certain point in this movement, some elements have gained predominance and others have disappeared or have become irrelevant within the general framework. Events that go under the specific name of 'crisis' have then burst onto the scene, events that are more or less serious according to whether more or less important elements of equilibrium come into play.[12]

Crises will ultimately lead to the death of capitalism, but each time – in the absence of an alternative, of a new life – they will 'immunize' it from the diseases and imbalances constantly faced by the dying order.[13] Having converted its economic crisis into

W. Streeck, *How Will Capitalism End? Essays on a Failing System*, London: Verso, 2016.

12 Gramsci, *Further Selections from the Prison Notebooks*, p. 353 [Q 15, § 5].

13 That a biopolitical lexicon circulated in the economic discourse of those years is proved by the fact that, in the midst of the crisis of 1929, Hermann Göring, who later became one of the prominent members of the Third Reich, pronounced these words during the meeting of the Reichstag on 10 May 1932 (therefore before the advent of Hitler): 'We compare the State economy to the bloodstream of the human body, and we must oppose with the utmost determination what still continues to draw blood from this body and thus leads it slowly but surely to death.' H. Göring, *Deutscher Reichstag*, 5. WP, pp. 2543 B-2543C (translation by SP). One could therefore define Nazism as a form of biopolitical immunization against the disease that struck the German body politic with the 1929 crisis. On Nazi biopolitics as the most radical expression of the immunitary *dispositif*, see R. Esposito, *Bíos:*

an art of government, capitalism – currently in its neoliberal form – rules for reasons of 'force majeure': 'the whole crisis is "due to *force majeure*", ... it is "structural" and not just due to the conjuncture'.[14]

Biopolitics and Philosophy, Minneapolis: University of Minnesota Press, 2008.
14   Gramsci, *Further Selections from the Prison Notebooks*, p. 357 [Q 14, § 57].

7

Philosophy of Crisis

The term 'philosophy of crisis' can be used to describe European philosophy between the two world wars, and included philosophers such as Edmund Husserl and Martin Heidegger.[1] These thinkers agreed with Gramsci that crisis did not produce 'something new' that could save the declining West and old Europe from inexorable decay. However, while Gramsci foresaw crisis as an art of government, for these thinkers, the condition of an inescapable crisis took on the form of nihilism.[2] For this reason, Gramsci cannot be considered a representative of the philosophy of crisis, which saw the only alternative to nihilism in the recovery of the Greek origin of the West, in

---

1 I borrow this definition of 'philosophy of crisis' and these considerations on the '*dispositif* of crisis' in European philosophy between the two world wars from R. Esposito, *A Philosophy for Europe: From the Outside*, Cambridge: Polity, 2018, chapter 1.

2 In Italy, the philosopher who revived the philosophy of crisis of the 1930s, while highlighting the system's rationality brought about by nihilism, was Massimo Cacciari, with his proposal of 'negative thought'. See M. Cacciari, *Krisis. Saggio sulla crisi del pensiero negativo da Nietzsche a Wittgenstein*, Milan: Feltrinelli, 1976.

the renewal of its mission, in a 'decision' that would rip the body of Europe from old age and death in order to let it drink from the fountain of youth, the fountain of a new beginning. Such a decision, however, corresponds to the judgment of crisis, which places the possibility of salvation in a return to the origin. Therefore, to escape from the crisis and to recover from the deadly disease of nihilism and relativism that had hit Europe, the philosophy of crisis relied on the *dispositif* of crisis that precluded the new. In this sense, I consider its manifesto to be Husserl's *The Crisis of European Sciences*. It is worth noting that, in order to be renewed, 'European humanity' – which for Husserl corresponded to humanity *tout court* – had to resort to philosophical criticism. This is not to determine the political decision in favour of the new, as in the young Marx's thought, but primarily to recover Europe's authentic origin. About a century after their alliance, the separation between criticism and decision is thus consummated:

> we as philosophers are heirs of the past in respect to the goals which the word 'philosophy' indicates, in terms of concepts, problems, and methods. What is clearly necessary ... is that we *reflect back*, in a thorough *historical* and *critical* fashion, in order to provide, *before all decisions*, for a radical self-understanding: we must inquire back into what was originally and always sought in philosophy ...; but this must include a critical consideration of what, in respect to the goals and methods [of philosophy], is ultimate, original, and genuine.[3]

---

3   E. Husserl, *The Crisis of European Sciences and Transcendental Phenomenology*, Evanston: Northwestern University Press, 1970, pp. 17–18.

Nor does the journal project promoted by Walter Benjamin and Bertolt Brecht at the end of 1930 and the beginning of 1931 fall within the 'philosophy of crisis'. In the aftermath of the first electoral successes of the National Socialist Party in Germany, Benjamin and Brecht tried to reunite the ultra-left German intelligentsia and – without claiming a vanguard position – put it at the service of the cause of communism and proletarian revolution. The magazine project was entitled 'Krise und Kritik'. Although they also recognized themselves as bourgeois intellectuals, unlike the 'philosophers of the crisis', Benjamin and Brecht intended to arm the proletariat with the weapons of criticism which had characterized the revolutionary character of bourgeois culture from the Enlightenment onwards. This programmatic intent is explicit in the 'Krise und Kritik' *Memorandum*:

> The journal is political. By that is meant that its critical activity is consciously anchored in the critical situation of present society – that of class struggle. At the same time, however, the journal will not be party political. It is emphatically not a proletarian paper, nor an organ of the proletariat. Rather will it fill the gap of a journal in which the bourgeois intelligentsia can do justice to itself through insights and challenges that, uniquely under current circumstances, permit it an active, interventionist role, with tangible consequences, as opposed to its usual ineffective arbitrariness.[4]

Repeating in a certain sense the gesture of the young Marx, the intention was to use criticism to reveal, if not to induce the

---

4   W. Benjamin, 'Krise und Kritik *Memorandum*', in E. Wizisla, *Walter Benjamin and Bertolt Brecht: Story of a Friendship*, New Haven: Yale University Press, 2009, p. 188.

birth of, the decisive crisis, which is latent and 'hidden' in the
overt decline of Western civilization. As we have shown, the
function of the crisis within the bourgeois capitalist system is
self-preservation, as is also indicated in the philosophy of crisis's call for a recovery of the origin. The decisive crisis – the
crisis stirred by the proletariat – is the goal, while the tools of
criticism are at the disposal of the bourgeois intelligentsia. In
the minutes of one of the journal's preparatory meetings, we
read: 'The journal's field of activity is the present *crisis* in all
areas of ideology, and it is the task of the journal to register
this crisis or to bring it about, and this by means of criticism.'[5]
The ideology mentioned here is precisely that of Heidegger's
school, which the journal proposed to 'annihilate'.[6] Crisis, as
understood by the philosophy of crisis, is ideological in essence:
by counterfeiting reality, it covers and mystifies the decisive
crisis. But criticism can be effective and incisive. As we learnt
from Koselleck, criticism is the most authentic legacy of bourgeois thought.

No issue of 'Krise und Kritik' was ever published, for several
reasons, the most important being that it was impossible to bring
together the different positions within the German ultra-leftist
intelligentsia (this problem deserves further reflection, as it re-
emerged at various times in the twentieth century). Another
reason, in some ways complementary to the first, was that the
interpretation of crisis at the time had not fully grasped the
extent to which the crisis had weakened the weapons of bourgeois criticism. The capitalist crisis of 1929 was, in fact, very
different from the 'crisis of bourgeois society', that political and

5   Quoted in Wizisla, *Walter Benjamin and Bertolt Brecht*, p. 76.
6   Ibid., p. 41.

moral crisis of authority in which criticism could actually intervene, because, as Koselleck reminds us, criticism had caused it.
The new crisis had a different nature to previous crises: bourgeois criticism no longer constituted a political critique within
it, just as the capitalist crisis was no longer inscribed within a
more general crisis of bourgeois society. A few decades later,
this separation finally became apparent: the movements and
critique of 1968 and the 1970s marked the culmination of the
crisis of bourgeois society (of its civilization and its culture);
in the same period, the crisis of Fordist capitalism initiated the
transformations of post-Fordist capitalism.

It is perhaps because he does not see the political and
economic crises as identical, but sees them as separate and
intertwined, that Gramsci could see an art of government in
the 'destiny' the West was choosing. He understood that the
new is not born by revitalizing the old, and neither can it be
generated from its death. The new does not originate within
the *dispositif* of crisis: it is neither an origin to recover nor a
condition to return to. As we shall see, the philosophy of crisis is
not the most effective way to recover the Greek connotation of
crisis. Instead, it would be within neoliberalism – in a probably
less conscious and certainly less refined way – that *krisis* would
become an effective *dispositif*.[7]

---

7   In his interpretation of neoliberalism, Massimo De Carolis finds in
the neoliberal 'model of civilization' the most effective answer – though its
inadequacy is now becoming apparent – to the crisis of modernity theorized
by the philosophy of crisis in the twentieth century. See M. De Carolis, *Il
rovescio della libertà. Tramonto del neoliberalismo e disagio della civiltà*, Mace-
rata: Quodlibet, 2017.

8
The Neoliberal Crisis

The Party of Life

A fundamental historical and conceptual shift occurred with the advent of neoliberalism: the *dispositif* of economic crisis became political in itself. Or rather, it has become a proper art of government. And, so, the modern idea of political crisis as a conflict leading to a 'final decision' has disappeared. As Walter Benjamin argued in his theses 'On the Concept of History',[1] the state of exception — which Carl Schmitt argued could only be

---

1 'The tradition of the oppressed teaches us that the "state of emergency" in which we live is not the exception but the rule.' W. Benjamin, 'On the Concept of History', in *Selected Writings, Volume 4, 1938–1940*, ed. H. Eiland and M.W. Jennings, Cambridge, MA: Harvard University Press, 2006, p. 392. The deeper and most explicit criticism of Schmitt's decisionist paradigm, however, is to be found in Benjamin's *The Origin of German Tragic Drama*, where the figure of the sovereign is modelled on Hamlet and on the representations of the tyrant/martyr typical of the seventeenth-century German *Trauerspiel*. The tragedy and fatal destiny of these figures derive from their inability to decide and their being irresolute, or from the fact that the solution of a final decision is impossible. It is worth recalling that Benjamin's theory of sovereignty in *The Origin of German Tragic Drama* is proposed in analogy with the political crisis of the Weimar Republic at the end of the 1920s.

brought to an end through the restoration of order in the 'final decision' of the sovereign[2] – had become the rule. Today, the 'state of exception as rule' no longer defines the predominance of the form of sovereign power but is part of the *dispositif* of economic crises that in politics corresponds to a form of administrative government: governmentality. No longer a condition of a possible decision in the crisis, conflict itself is *governed* by crisis, since it aims at a 'decision' which is always already preordained. The decision is therefore converted into a choice that is always in *response* to the crisis, that is to say it cannot be separated from the functioning of the *dispositif* in which it is inscribed: the alternative posed by the crisis is fictitious – the choice is expressed when it is clear that there is no choice. Rather than being final, every decision leads to a new distinction and, by imposing new choices, to a new crisis – and so on ad infinitum.

The temporality of the crisis has now been completely converted into a cyclical pattern: we live in the 'eternal repetition of the present', a present devoid even of the unknown land represented by the future, by the possibility of alternatives. This completes the neoliberal revolution announced by Thatcher in the 1980s with the slogan 'There is no alternative' (TINA), meaning that socialism was not an alternative to the market economy.[3] The neoliberal denotation of the expression

---

2   Schmitt's definition of sovereignty is well-known: 'Sovereign is he who decides on the exception.' C. Schmitt, *Political Theology: Four Chapters on the Concept of Sovereignty*, Cambridge, MA: MIT Press, 1985, p. 5.

3   On the model of 'socialist realism', Mark Fisher invented the term 'capitalist realism' to define the neoliberal condition based on the idea that 'there is no alternative'. See M. Fisher, *Capitalist Realism: Is There No Alternative?*, Winchester: Zero Books, 2009.

'there is no alternative' is similar to the meaning intended by its creator, Herbert Spencer, who argued that, to have an order, a society must have laws that reflect those of the universe: 'sure, inflexible, ever active, and having no exceptions'.[4] The neoliberal revolution indeed recovered and reactivated the pre-modern and astronomical meaning of the term 'revolution' – a legacy which, as we saw above, was still very present in Rousseau. Natural cycles, repetition, and the stability of the established order regain their temporal primacy over the historicity and progressive linearity of the modern notion of time. The temporality of the neoliberal crisis is then fully inscribed within a 'natural history' determined by the absence of alternatives. With the neoliberal crisis we return to the circularity of 'diagnosis' and 'prognosis' that for Koselleck was broken by the irruption into history of modern temporality and of revolution as the affirmation of the new and discontinuity with the past. Hence the return to the temporality of the 'future past': 'Political prognostication also had a static temporal structure, insofar as it operated in terms of natural magnitudes whose potential repeatability formed the cyclical character of its history. The prognosis implies a diagnosis which introduces the past into the future.'[5]

The neoliberal revolution is, therefore, a 'revolution/ restoration', which could be defined under Gramsci's category of 'passive revolution'. It consists in

---

4   H. Spencer, *Social Statics: or, The Conditions Essential to Human Happiness Specified, and the First of them Developed*, New York: D. Appleton and Company, 1883, p. 55.
5   R. Koselleck, *Futures Past: On the Semantics of Historical Time*, New York: Columbia University Press, 2004, p. 22.

the historical fact that a unitary popular initiative was missing ... together with the other fact that this development took place as the reaction of the dominant classes to the sporadic, elementary and non-organic rebelliousness of the popular masses together with 'restorations' that accepted a certain part of the demands expressed from below, and were thus 'progressive restorations' or 'revolutions-restorations' or even 'passive revolutions'.[6]

Yet before Thatcher's slogan could characterize a *dispositif* of the crisis as a direct, immediate, and affirmative art of government,[7] neoliberalism took another fundamental step. It turned the judgment of *krisis* into a form of political judgment, in fact making it the political judgment par excellence. The *krinein*, which in the Greek world characterized the judgment of the law and medicine, now enters politics. If, for Plato and Hippocrates, the *krinein* of the judge and the physician was *at the service* of political power, this mode of judgment now constitutes the art of neoliberal government, which we will call 'biopolitics'. And the neoliberal crisis can be defined as a 'biopolitical crisis'. Although it is presented and presents itself as an economic crisis, this crisis in fact functions as a *dispositif* of government and has a full governmental function in producing and regulating the conduct of forms of life. Thatcher herself claimed, 'Economics are the method: the object is to change the soul.'[8]

---

6   Gramsci, *Further Selections from the Prison Notebooks*, p. 523 [Q 10, § 41].
7   There are several different examples, from a variety of countries, of crisis as art of government. Despite the differences due to the context, the formula with which crisis ultimately legitimates particularly unpopular decrees or even the formation of new governments ('technical' governments are the most exemplary case) is basically the same: 'there is no alternative'.
8   M. Thatcher, interview with *The Sunday Times*, 3 May 1981.

The neoliberal art of government shapes individuals' conduct and transforms their souls through constant judgment. Unlike in Plato, for the judgment to be correct their souls cannot be separated from their bodies and their way of life. On the contrary, the judgment has to intervene in forms of life. Thus, the court of the Last Judgment is no longer final, but instead becomes the 'rule'. Crisis as art of government acts directly on the souls of individuals, on their 'living' soul. Life – the soul, the form of life, the conduct of life – is the real object of neoliberalism and of its politics. While the class party used to determine the class struggle, thereby becoming the expression of the modern conception of conflict (with its solution in the decision), the 'party of life' is the expression of the neoliberal art of government.

Friedrich A. von Hayek used the expression 'party of life', when trying to find a name for his conception of liberalism that would distinguish it from previous conceptions. Hayek writes: 'What I should want is a word which describes the party of life, the party that favors free growth and spontaneous evolution.'[9] Here, for the first time, life – its preservation and promotion – becomes the prerogative of a *political party*. The 'party of life' considers life as a prerogative of its own side, offering itself – in the name of life – as an alternative, in conflict with the prerogatives of other social groups. However, it is, at the same time, 'impartial': there can be no alternatives to the party of life. The moment in which a politics of life takes on the form of a 'party of life', it produces and implies its opposite: the party or parties that threaten the survival of the political and social body. Once

---

9   F. A. von Hayek, 'Why I Am Not a Conservative', in *The Constitution of Liberty*, Chicago: Chicago University Press, 2011 [1960], p. 530.

again, the side to be taken does not appear as a choice between feasible alternatives. In the form of the 'party of life', therefore, biopolitics acquires its most authentically neoliberal trait. With the 'party of life', Hayek takes to the extreme an idea that his mentor Ludwig von Mises also attributed to liberalism as the 'program of a party's economic policy'.[10] In *Human Action*, Mises argues that liberalism 'presupposes that people prefer life to death, health to sickness, nourishment to starvation, abundance to poverty'.[11] But we cannot ignore the fact that this biopolitical declination of liberalism reveals the difference between neoliberalism itself and the classical liberal tradition. As emerges several times in his autobiography,[12] Hayek's economic and social doctrine was inspired by evolutionism,[13]

10　See the entry by von Mises 'Wirtschaftlicher Liberalismus' (Economic Liberalism), in *Handwörterbuch der Sozialwissenschaften*, Vol. 6, Stuttgart-Tübingen-Göttingen: Fischer/Mohr/Vandenhoeck & Ruprecht, 1959, pp. 596–603.

11　L. von Mises, *Human Action: A Treatise on Economics*, San Francisco: Fox & Wilkes, 1996 [1949], p. 154.

12　See F.A. Hayek, *Hayek on Hayek: An Autobiographical Dialogue*, ed. S. Kresge and L. Wenar, Chicago: University of Chicago Press, 1994.

13　It should be noted that Hayek does not consider the concept of 'evolution' as originally belonging to the field of biology because, if that were the case, if it concerned exclusively the individual, it would not have the capacity to affect society and the 'population': 'There are, of course, important differences between the manner in which the process of selection operates in the cultural transmission that leads to the formation of social institutions, and the manner in which it operates in the selection of innate biological characteristics and their transmission by physiological inheritance ... But although the scheme of Darwinian theory has only limited application to the [former] and its literal use leads to grave distortions, the basic conception of evolution is still the same in both fields.' F.A. Hayek, *Law, Legislation and Liberty: A New Statement of the Liberal Principles of Justice and Political Economy*, Abingdon: Routledge, 2013, p. 23. For an analysis of the link between political economy and biology in the current stage of neoliberalism, see M. Cooper, *Life as Surplus: Biotechnology and Capitalism in the Neoliberal Era*, Seattle: University of Washington Press, 2008.

which influenced both his party of life and the biopolitics that stemmed from it.

Strong biopolitical traits are already evident in Friedrich Nietzsche, the philosopher who coined the expression 'party of life'. According to Nietzsche, the party of life would be tasked with 'big politics', which corresponds to biopolitics, or a politics that, to 'breed humanity as a whole', cannot grant alternatives. Big politics is, on the one hand, a 'guarantee for life' and for life's empowerment, but as a party it also determines the opposite party, that challenges life and limits its power: 'to create a party of life, strong enough for big politics: the big politics makes the physiology of the mistress of all other issues – it wants [humanity] as a whole breed, it measures the rank of the breeds, of the peoples, of the individuals according to their future – by its guarantee for life, which it carries in itself – it does with everything degenerates and parasitic inexorably to an end'.[14] It is, however, Ernst Nolte, who, in *Nietzsche und der Nietzscheanismus*, gives the most prominence – even more than Nietzsche – to the expression 'party of life', in order to identify the opposite party: Marx's 'class party'.[15]

As evidence that the distance between Hayek and Nolte is not as great as it might first seem, both thinkers were awarded the Hanns Martin Schleyer-Preis in 1985, an award conferred on those whose contribution 'consolidates and strengthens the

---

14   F. Nietzsche, *Nietzsche's Last Notebooks 1888*, p. 258 [25/1], at archive. org (translation modified). In the same year (1888) and almost with the same words, Nietzsche uses the expression 'party of life' in *Ecce homo*. See F. Nietzsche, *Ecce Homo: How to Become What You Are*, Oxford: Oxford University Press, 2007, p. 48.

15   See E. Nolte, *Nietzsche und der Nietzscheanismus*, Frankfurt a.M: Ullstein-Verlag, 1990.

foundations of a community based on the principle of individual freedom'. The speech Hayek gave upon receiving the award – entitled 'Die Überheblichkeit der Vernunft' (The Presumption of Reason) – is also revealing. It was not directly economic, but referred explicitly to a theory of evolution on which all knowledge and all morals (especially traditional morality) were based, with a heuristic outcome regarding the human being as such: 'I believe we are on the way to seeing the development of reason as a process of evolution, we are even in the process of developing an evolutionary theory of knowledge. We can also prove that the moral tradition is not born as a product of reason, but rather as a similar evolutionary process.'[16] Hayek understands the morality that results from this evolutionary process as the prerogative of one party that is opposed to another, allowing no alternatives. The 'life' of Hayek's party is therefore life as conceived in an evolutionary theory:

> current controversies about what is moral, about what morality requires us to do, are not a fight about given morals, but a struggle between two completely different moral traditions ... The struggle between capitalism and socialism is not a struggle on the basis of given morals. It is a conflict between two entirely different morals, one of which usually succumbs, because we never consciously conceived it and therefore we cannot justify or explain it, but it is the one that has shaped our existence ... Both parties claim to be in favour of freedom. And freedom contains two completely different

---

16   F.A. Hayek, 'Die Überheblichkeit der Vernunft', in *Hanns Martin Schleyer-Preis 1984 und 1985*, Cologne: Hanns Martin Schleyer-Stiftung, 1985, p. 50 (translation by SP). Nolte's speech is entitled: '*Über den historischen Begriff des "Liberalen System"*' (*On the Concept of 'Liberal System'*).

things: the classical moral tradition has produced a free society, in which it persuaded the human being to repress certain primitive instincts ... It faces today a new movement, which calls itself 'liberation', which requires us to get rid of these stupid limitations, due to religion, to finally pursue our feelings and our ambitions.[17]

Hayek's 'party of life' is opposed to another party which in those years supported a universal and comprehensive claim – the class party, or socialism – but, unlike the latter, its utopia is not progressive, but conservative. 'Conservative utopia' may seem to be an oxymoron if the term 'utopia' is used in the modern sense, as a temporality pointing towards the future. Instead, the neoliberal utopia that Hayek's conception helps to build finds its force neither in progress nor in Enlightenment reason; it is instead oriented to predict and pre-empt the future. The future is determined by the evolution of society as it adapts towards order.[18] And evolution's rationality – unintelligible a priori – is the sole prerogative of order. Society and its members are not called upon to transform order, claiming presumptuously that they know it, but must 'limit' themselves to preserve it.

It is now necessary to correct and clarify the common discourse about neoliberalism, which holds that its peculiarity is the promotion of the potential of the human being as human in order to make it profitable. Unlike for Nietzsche, for Hayek this must include the limitation of 'primitive instincts'. The

---

17   Ibid., pp. 51–2 (translation by SP).
18   Melinda Cooper pointed out the close link between neoliberalism (Hayek's and in general) and neoconservatism. See her *Family Values: Between Neoliberalism and the New Social Conservatism*, New York: Zone Books, 2017.

promotion of the potential of the human being as such is part of the *dispositif* of neoliberal government, but, following Hayek, we must consider it inseparable from another aspect which is equally critical to the functioning of this *dispositif*: the investment in forms of life needs to be inscribed at the same time within an order to be preserved, so that the changes required by the evolution of forms of life must help to preserve the order.

Hayek's fundamental contribution to the configuration of the *dispositif* of neoliberal government is his definition of this order as 'cosmos'. Among other things, it is precisely this 'cosmic' conception of the market order that distinguishes the neoliberalism inspired by Hayek and the so-called Austrian School from 'ordoliberalism'. According to Alexander Rüstow, one of the prominent exponents of ordoliberalism, classical liberalism's inadequacy stems from the theory of the 'invisible hand' – which according to Adam Smith governs and ensures the harmonization between the individual's selfish interests and the collective well-being in the dynamic of the market. This idea can be traced back to the cosmology of Pythagoras and the religiosity of ancient Greece. For Rüstow, this 'invisible harmony' of the cosmos of the market represents a theological-metaphysical legacy that led to liberalism being defeated by Nazism and communism in the 1930s, and which would be rejected in the model of neoliberalism that he promoted.[19] For

---

19   See A. Rüstow, *Die Religion der Marktwirtschaft*, Berlin: Lit Verlag, 2009 [1949]. The cosmic religiosity underlying the capitalist vision of the world should not however be understood in the theological-dogmatic sense, but – as Hayek does – as a 'cult', since it conditions and governs the practical conduct of individuals. By radicalizing Max Weber's thought, who identified the source of the spirit of capitalism in Protestant ethics, Walter Benjamin

Hayek, on the other hand, it is precisely the rationality of the cosmos – presupposed and yet inscrutable for the individuals who act in the market – that configures the market's spontaneous order. And the project of his neoliberalism was to turn this cosmic faith of classical liberalism into the utopia of a party of life.

We have to take the utopian focus that Foucault attached to Hayek's proposal with the caveat that it is a conservative utopia, like any pre-modern utopia. This utopian focus makes the neoliberal project diverse and global. Drawing on the binary logic of a still modern political crisis playing out within mid-twentieth-century conflicts, Hayek presents his 'liberal utopia' as the alternative to the socialist utopia that was dominant at the time: 'What we lack is a liberal Utopia, a program that seems neither a mere defence of things as they are nor a diluted kind of socialism, but a truly liberal radicalism.'[20] Paraphrasing this passage by Hayek, Foucault understood that neoliberalism could prevail not so much because it represented a political or governmental alternative – as if it were a party against or amongst others – but because its *dispositif* was a real *dispositif* of 'biopolitical governmentality'. Its peculiarity was, therefore, to promote an order that does not present itself as an alternative to the established order, but as the only possible one:

---

defines capitalism as 'a purely cultic religion, perhaps the most extreme that ever existed'. W. Benjamin, 'Capitalism as Religion', in *Selected Writings, Volume 1, 1916–1926*, ed. M. Bullock and M.W. Jennings, Cambridge, MA: Harvard University Press, 1996, p. 288.

20   F.A. Hayek, 'Intellectuals and Socialism' [1949], in *Studies in Philosophy, Politics and Economics*, Chicago: University of Chicago Press, 1967, p. 194.

I think this is why American liberalism currently appears not just, or not so much as a political alternative, but let's say as a sort of many-sided, ambiguous, global claim with a foothold in both the right and the left. It is also a sort of utopian focus which is always being revived … Some years ago Hayek said: We need a liberalism that is a living thought. Liberalism has always left it to the socialists to produce utopias, and socialism owes much of its vigor and historical dynamism to this utopian or utopia-creating activity. Well, liberalism also needs utopia. It is up to us to create liberal utopias, to think in a liberal mode, rather than presenting liberalism as a technical alternative for government. Liberalism must be a general style of thought, analysis, and imagination.[21]

In Hayek's terms, the neoliberal utopia does not mean simply minimizing the interference of state and government in the free market and economic affairs, as is commonly understood, for this would simply place it in continuity with the liberal tradition. The desire expressed in the neoliberal utopia goes further, considering the state as a private enterprise among others, involved in competition between private companies (the so-called governance), aimed at leaving no space for political alternatives.[22] Therefore, in conceiving of the state as an enterprise like any

---

21   M. Foucault, *The Birth of Biopolitics: Lectures at the Collège de France, 1978–1979*, Basingstoke: Palgrave Macmillan, 2008, pp. 218–19.

22   The passage by Hayek which Foucault paraphrases is even more powerful and radical in the original, with tones typical of a real political manifesto: 'What we lack is a liberal Utopia, a programme which seems neither a mere defence of things as they are nor a diluted kind of socialism, but a truly liberal radicalism … The practical compromises they must leave to the politicians. Free trade and freedom of opportunity are ideals which still may arouse the imaginations of large numbers, but a mere "reasonable freedom of trade" or a mere "relaxation of controls" is neither intellectually respectable nor likely to inspire any enthusiasm.' Hayek, 'Intellectuals and Socialism', p. 194.

other,[23] the neoliberal utopia attaches the prerogatives of politics to the free market, prerogatives that include the autonomy that allows it to govern itself *juxta propria principia*. In fact, if the doctrines of early liberalism – elaborated in England and Scotland in the seventeenth and eighteenth centuries – 'perfectly fit the content of the state's activity, but not the form of government',[24] the 'new liberalism' needed first of all to deal with the question of 'government' if it wanted to take on a political connotation: 'The new liberalism is distinguished from the old liberalism, above all because of the greater awareness, now acquired, of the very close mutual nexus that exists between political and economic institutions.'[25] In other words, with neoliberalism, the form of government was no longer the prerogative of the state but was produced by the market. In neoliberal thought, therefore, the role of the state depends not on how much it can intervene in market dynamics, but on the 'function' that it has in the government of the market. This function became apparent in the aftermath of the 2007/8 crisis, when states saved banks from bankruptcy, and above all with the austerity policies that followed the so-called public debt crisis. These policies, far from being a form of regulation of an out-of-control market, were instead entirely implicated in the temporal logic of the risk that characterizes 'financial speculation', since they ended up guaranteeing the stability of the order, ensuring the return and collection of investments.[26] Moreover, even

---

23   'But what is objectionable here is not state enterprise as such but state monopoly.' F.A. Hayek, *The Constitution of Liberty*, p. 334.

24   F.A. Hayek, 'Politischer Liberalismus', in *Handwörterbuch der Sozialwissenschaften*, Vol. 6, p. 592 (translation by SP).

25   Ibid., p. 595.

26   See M. Konings, *Capital and Time: For a New Critique of Neoliberal Reason*, Stanford: Stanford University Press, 2018.

more recently, it has become clear that the function of the state in the neoliberal order does not exclude authoritarian drifts. The 'return of the state', to which people from both the right and the left refer when talking about the rise of so-called 'new populisms', is not incompatible with neoliberalism. Adapting existing definitions of crisis to the current political scenario, we can see that the 'imperfect crisis' of the 'new populisms', with the resumption of the figure of the charismatic leader and the need for a strong state, is not a consequence of nor an alternative to the 'perfect crisis' of neoliberalism, but is part of it and one of its functions.[27] It should also not be forgotten that the first country to adopt neoliberal policies was Pinochet's Chile. Speaking on Pinochet in 1981, Hayek declared to a Chilean newspaper: 'it is possible for a dictator to govern in a liberal way. And it is also possible for a democracy to govern with a total lack of liberalism. Personally I prefer a liberal dictator to democratic government lacking liberalism.'[28] In sum, contrary to what we are given to think, there is no binding and exclusive link between the neoliberal market and democracy. The market demands the political regime that is most functional to its order in the given circumstances, and today, more than ever, that regime is authoritarian.[29]

---

27   David Harvey has already pointed out the reactionary and authoritarian character of neoliberalism in relation to nationalism: 'the neoliberal state needs nationalism of a certain sort to survive'. D. Harvey, *A Brief History of Neoliberalism*, Oxford: Oxford University Press, 2005, p. 85. Moreover, as argued by William Davies, nationalism ended up being perfectly compatible with the neoliberal principle of competitiveness in the economic and political form of 'national competitiveness'. See W. Davies, *The Limits of Neoliberalism: Authority, Sovereignty and the Logic of Competition*, London: SAGE, 2017.

28   Interview in *El Mercurio*, 12 April 1981.

29   See W. Brown, *In the Ruins of Neoliberalism: The Rise of Antidemocratic Politics in the West*, New York: Columbia University Press, 2019.

Hayek was well aware that a conception of the spontaneous order of the market as having governmental prerogatives could not be reduced to an economic discourse. In fact, after his initial works he abandoned his reflections on economy in the strict sense. Those first works were written in the 1930s when his economic reflection was obviously focused on the 1929 crisis, on its causes and possible solutions. In texts such as *Monetary Theory and the Trade Cycle* (1933) and *Prices and Production* (1935), Hayek addressed the issue of crisis within the theory of general economic equilibrium, adopting the 'classical' scheme of crisis as imbalance with the recovery of the economic cycle restoring balance. It was in these years that Hayek started his polemic against Keynesianism that he maintained throughout his life. At the time, the Keynesian concept of the New Deal prevailed, and Hayek's ideas were temporarily repressed. In the same period, Karl Polanyi argued that with the crisis of 1929 the classical liberal idea of market self-regulation had disappeared, which brought about the need for a 'new utopia' and for a 'great transformation'.[30] Hayek came to similar conclusions in his own work, using the defeat suffered by Keynesianism in terms of economic strategies for dealing with the crisis as the premise for a counteroffensive launched on a grand scale.

Hayek understood that the game could not be played on the 'technical' ground of economics. His defeat by Keynesianism resulted from his reducing the crisis to the problem of restoring equilibrium in economic cycles, excluding the problem of the 'government' of the crisis. Therefore, the market and its cycles were no longer to be considered on the basis of balance, but

---

30   See K. Polanyi, *The Great Transformation: The Political and Economic Origins of Our Time*, Boston: Beacon Press, 2001.

according to the principle of *order*. From the 1940s onwards, fully aware of the application of evolutionary theory to the social sciences, Hayek defined the market as a 'spontaneous order'. Subsequently, in the third volume of *Law, Legislation and Liberty* (1979), he gave a further clarification that explains the meaning of 'spontaneous order': 'Though I still like and occasionally use the term "spontaneous order," I agree that "self-generating order" or "self-organizing structures" are sometimes more precise and unambiguous and therefore frequently use them instead of the former term. Similarly, instead of "order," in conformity with today's predominant usage, I occasionally now use "system."'[31] The spontaneous order of the market was thus a form of government in all respects, which contained its own principle of order and, therefore, was self-generating, self-regulating, and self-organizing. A purely economic definition of the market had not made it fully explicit that its order was an order of government, a *cosmos*:

> The spontaneous order of the market, based on reciprocity or mutual benefits, is commonly described as an economic order ... But it is exceedingly misleading, and has become one of the chief sources of confusion and misunderstanding, to call this order an economy as we do when we speak of a national, social, or world economy ... I propose that we call this spontaneous order of the market a catallaxy in analogy to the term 'catallactics', which has often been proposed as a substitute for the term 'economics'. (Both 'catallaxy' and 'catallactics' derived from the ancient Greek verb *katallattein* which, significantly, means not only 'to barter' and 'to

---

31   F.A. Hayek, *Law, Legislation and Liberty*, *Volume 3: The Political Order of a Free People*, Chicago: University of Chicago Press, 1981, p. xii.

exchange', but also 'to admit into the community' and 'to turn from enemy into friend'.)[32]

The term 'catallaxy' had already been introduced in the lexicon of the Austrian School by Hayek's mentor, Ludwig von Mises. For Mises, however, 'catallactics' indicates the narrow scope of specifically economic problems, thus defining the analysis of actions taken on the basis of monetary calculation, and it is 'praxeology' instead that defines economics as a general science of all human action.[33] It is thus Hayek who first understands catallaxy not only as including economics in a wider sense than that of simple monetary calculation, but also as a real capability to govern. Indeed, on the basis of the word's Greek etymology, which Hayek himself refers to, to attach a 'catallactic' quality to the spontaneous order of the market means to conceive the exchange economy as immediately endowed with a 'governance' that is able – according to the other meaning of the verb *katallattein* – to 'reconcile, to cease hostilities, war, and conflict'.

But what kind of 'reconciliation' does catallaxy guarantee? Like its Greek root, it is still an 'exchange' – between interests, profits, benefits – that is carried out in order to encourage a

---

32   F.A. Hayek, 'The Principles of a Liberal Social Order' [1966], in *Studies in Philosophy, Politics and Economics*, Routledge edition, p. 164. On catallaxy, see also Hayek, *Law, Legislation and Liberty*, pp. 267–90.

33   Mises's famous definition of economics as praxeology, critical to the development of the Austrian School – including Hayek himself – and of neo-liberalism as the government of conducts, is as follows: 'Praxeology does not deal with the external world, but with man's conduct with regard to it. Praxeological reality is not the physical universe, but man's conscious reaction to the given state of this universe. Economics is not about things and tangible material objects; it is about men, their meanings and actions.' Von Mises, *Human Action*, p. 92.

cessation of hostilities. The reconciliation brought about by catallaxy does not extinguish conflict or war, but suspends it in the
name of an interest which, while not superior, is simply more
advantageous at a given moment. Catallaxy does not create a
political community, but its policy is always dictated and determined by a particular interest. In light of this, I draw from one
of the most authoritative sources in ancient Greece, to which
Hayek himself also points, in order to elaborate the 'political'
use of the verb *katallattein*. In a passage by Thucydides, in his
History of the Peloponnesian War, the Syracusan Hermocrates
talks to the Sicilian people and urges them to cease the hostilities between Sicilian cities, on the grounds that in their present
circumstances a 'reconciliation' would be preferable to war and
more in their interests, because they needed to fight another
war, against the Athenians, which would be more advantageous
to them:

> As for the miseries which war entails, why should one by expressly
> stating all that can be said make a long harangue in the presence of
> those who know? For no one is either forced to make war through
> ignorance of what it is, or deterred from making it by fear, if he
> thinks he will get some advantage from it. What really happens
> is this, that to one side the gains appear greater than the terrors,
> while the other deliberately prefers to undergo the dangers rather
> than submit to a temporary disadvantage; but if it should turn out
> that these two lines of action are both inopportune, each for the
> side which adopts it, then some profit may come from exhortations
> which advise a compromise. And so with us at the present time, if
> we could be persuaded of the wisdom of this course it would be to
> our great advantage; for each of us began the war in the first place

because we desired to promote our private interests. So now let us endeavour by setting forth our conflicting claims to become reconciled (*katallagénai*) with each other; and then, if we do not after all succeed in securing, each of us, what is fair and just before we part, we shall go to war again.[34]

The political order defined by catallaxy is based on the principle of creating the greatest gains for those involved, always through an exchange between different private interests. It does not eliminate conflict, but modifies it from time to time, on a case-by-case basis, according to the requirements of the moment. This mobility and constant displacement of conflict – through reshaping existing subjects and parties and at the same time identifying new and different ones – could be defined in terms of *competition*. The politics of catallaxy does not aim at the creation of communities but consists in subjugating conflict and its power to the logic of creating the greatest advantage and greatest benefit at any given time – this is the 'political' logic of the market. In the market, modern political conflict – class conflict, or, more generally, according to Carl Schmitt's classical formulation, the conflict between friend and enemy[35] – is made

---

34   Thucydides, *History of Peloponnesian War*, Vol. II, ed. C. Forster Smith, London: William Heinemann, 1920, p. 311 [4, 59].

35   Hayek is very aware of the comparison with Schmitt's legal concept of 'friend-enemy', to which he refers in particular in *Law, Legislation, Liberty* (p. 68). The fundamental 'political' act of catallaxy consists in the conversion of the 'political enemy' into the 'economic competitor' that collaborates in the conservation of the Great Society: 'That we assist in the realization of other people's aims without sharing them or even knowing them, and solely in order to achieve our own aims, is the source of strength of the Great Society. So long as collaboration presupposes common purposes, people with different aims are necessarily enemies who may fight each other for the same means.' Ibid., p. 270.

precarious, diffused and so neutralized in the form of competition, which ends up working as a social link within what Hayek calls the global Great Society. The neutralization of political conflict – 'to cease hostilities and war' – is the condition for the competition that governs the catallactic order of the market. And so the party of life prevails over the class party.

Judgment without Justice

In catallaxy, there is no political government which could potentially be an alternative to market self-regulation. On the contrary, state policy must depend on government by the market: the state is no longer the main actor and the primary form of politics.[36] This does not mean that government by the market is not supported by an order, just that this order has no political 'end'. The catallactic order of the market carries with it a different politics.[37] According to Hayek, politics has no space to intervene outside the market, in the name of justice or out of respect for a common goal, to balance or imbalance the given order, and thus to govern conflicts or to promote them:

36　It is in the function of the state considered as a private entity among others, and yet called to impose with its legislative activity the logic of private law at every level, that Pierre Laval and Christian Dardot identify the peculiarities of Hayek's contribution to 'neoliberal' rationality and the most radical break with classical liberalism. See P. Dardot and C. Laval, *The New Way of the World: On Neoliberal Society*, London: Verso, 2013 [2009].

37　It is generally said that the two schools of neoliberalism – German ordoliberalism and the Austro-American neoliberalism led by Hayek – diverge on the role they assign to the state. Ordoliberalism implies the intervention of the state to safeguard the market from lobbies and monopolistic concentrations, thus re-establishing a 'social market economy'. For Hayek, instead, this 'political' function is produced from within the dynamics of the market itself. For a history of neoliberalism, see Q. Slobodian, *Globalists: The End of Empire and the Birth of Neoliberalism*, Cambridge, MA: Harvard University Press, 2018.

The belief that there can be no rational policy without a common scale of concrete ends implies, however, an interpretation of the catallaxy as an economy proper and for this reason is misleading. Policy need not be guided by the striving for the achievement of particular results, but may be directed towards securing an abstract overall order of such character that it will secure for the members the best chance of achieving their different and largely unknown particular ends.[38]

Justice itself cannot represent a society's common end or be a precondition for any political community. Just as politics' autonomy from the market is reduced, so too is justice brought entirely within *common law*, which is expected to perform the basic function of 'governing' individuals' conduct or, in other words, governing the 'population' as a group of individuals engaged in the pursuit of their own particular aims.[39] If 'social justice' is a senseless expression for Hayek, justice is not excluded from the order of the market: 'But it is justice in this sense which courts of justice administer and which is the original meaning of justice and must govern men's conduct if peaceful coexistence of free men is to be possible ... [J]ustice in the sense of rules of just conduct is indispensable for the intercourse of free men.'[40] This is a complete reversal of the Platonic approach: the court decides on justice without the need to be legitimized by politics. The same reversal is seen in the

---

38   Hayek, *Law, Legislation and Liberty*, p. 114.
39   In medieval English law, a court of equity was supposed to guarantee a sort of social or material justice; citizens could appeal to it to request that the judgments of the common law courts be repealed or amended. Later, the law of equity was included in the common law.
40   Hayek, *Law, Legislation and Liberty*, p. 259.

prominence Hayek attributes to the 'judge' over the 'legislator' or – as Plato would have it – over the 'statesman':

> It has already been pointed out that the ideal of individual liberty
> seems to have flourished chiefly among people where, at least
> for long periods, judge-made law predominated. This we have
> ascribed to the circumstance that judge-made law will of necessity
> possess certain attributes which the decrees of the legislator need
> not possess and are likely to possess only if the legislator takes
> judge-made law for his model.[41]

The judges are not asked to produce or create an order, to piece
together a 'constitution': they have no 'constituent power';
they do not 'posit' the law, rather, they 'find the law' inside an
assumed order, through the standards of individual conduct on
which, from time to time and always in special cases, they must
express their judgment. The order produces the standards of
conduct, not vice versa. The judge has to correct deviations
and deviances in conduct, bringing them back to the order, to
the *norm*.[42] The order evolves like an organism[43] because it

---

41   Ibid., p. 90.

42   Alain Supiot argues that Hayek perverts the *common law* into 'normative Darwinism', according to which the law ends up being founded on free
competition (and not vice versa), thus favouring the 'selection of rules and
practices' that best fit the order of the market. See A. Supiot, *Governance by
Numbers: The Making of a Legal Model of Allegiance*, London: Bloomsbury,
2017 [2015].

43   In fact, Hayek refuses an 'organicist' conception of the spontaneous
order, rejecting the hierarchical and fixed character of the that conception's
functions: 'Organisms are indeed a kind of spontaneous order and as such
show many of the characteristics of other spontaneous orders. It was therefore
tempting to borrow such terms as "growth," "adaptation," and "function"
from them … The chief peculiarity of organisms which distinguishes them
from the spontaneous orders of society is that in an organism most of the

self-regulates for self-preservation: conduct must be oriented towards the preservation of the order. Individual conduct – even if initially eccentric – should be put at the service of the order. This is the function of the judge: 'The contention that the judges by their decisions of particular cases gradually approach a system of rules of conduct which is most conducive to producing an efficient order of actions becomes more plausible when it is realized that this is in fact merely the same kind of process as that by which all intellectual evolution proceeds.'[44] Although differing from case to case, the judgment of the court is always oriented towards the confirmation, endorsement, and legitimation of the order. Therefore, in the spontaneous order, justice corresponds to justness of conduct, that is, to its adjustments to the order. From Plato onwards, it is 'justness' that is asked of the judgment of the court, but with Hayek this judgement, while based on 'justness', does not necessarily presuppose justice. The judgment of the court instead has the function of 'adapting' society from time to time to changing circumstances, so that the exogenous transformations that will naturally intervene in society are converted into endogenous ones, that is,

---

individual elements occupy fixed places which, at least once the organism is mature, they retain once and for all.' Hayek, *Law, Legislation and Liberty*, p. 50. Hayek lacked a term like biopolitics, where the preservation of the order is produced through the promotion of individual stances that contribute to the self-organization and self-generation of the spontaneous order. However, he looked with interest at cybernetics and, if we translate the self-organizing system of cybernetics into a form of government ('cybernetics' derives from the Greek *kybernetike techne*, which means 'art of government'), we can see the premises for the shift to biopolitics: 'Only recently has there arisen within the physical sciences under the name of cybernetics a special discipline which is also concerned with what are called self-organizing or self-generating systems.' Ibid., p. 36.

44   Ibid., p. 112.

are oriented towards the preservation of the order. This order, therefore, evolves through its own preservation: 'The efforts of the judge are thus part of that process of adaptation of society to circumstances by which the spontaneous order grows.'[45] For Hayek, the model par excellence of the spontaneous order is the market. The market is subject neither to political criteria nor to justice, and its criterion is self-preservation: 'although the judge is not committed to upholding a particular *status quo*, he is committed to upholding the principles on which the existing order is based. His task is indeed one which has meaning only within a spontaneous and abstract order of actions such as the market produces.'[46]

Hayek uses the word *nomos* to refer to the law of the judges, which governs the rules of individual conduct. Thus, *nomos*, the same Greek word that for Carl Schmitt founds sovereign power on earth, for Hayek, by contrast, indicates the governmental power that administers the order of the market by setting the rules of conduct for individuals and the population.[47] My point here is not to locate, through a certain interpretation of Plato and Schmitt, an alternative to neoliberal governmentality in a return to sovereign power. Far from it, I want to show how Hayek completely lacks the Platonic distinctions between justice and law and between judicial decision and political decision, a lack which, starting from Foucault, allows us to speak of biopolitics as the predominant form of government. This lack

---

45   Ibid., p. 113.

46   Ibid., p. 114.

47   For a critique of both Schmitt's sovereign 'nomos' and that of the neoliberal market, see F. Luisetti, J. Pickles, and W. Kaiser (eds.), *The Anomie of the Earth: Philosophy, Politics, and Autonomy in Europe and the Americas*, Durham, NC: Duke University Press, 2015.

of distinction also makes it possible to elevate crisis and its mode of judgment – which Plato had excluded from the scope of politics – to an art of government. This elevation of the ongoing neoliberal crisis that governs through forced decisions, which establishes itself when 'there is no alternative', was predicted by Hayek at the end of *Law, Legislation and Liberty*: 'What I have been trying to sketch in these volumes … has been a guide out of the process of degeneration of the existing form of government, and to construct an intellectual emergency equipment which will be available when we have no choice but to replace the tottering structure by some better edifice rather than resort in despair to some sort of dictatorial regime.'[48] If the alternative to the spontaneous order of the market is a dictatorship, then – once again – there is no alternative, the choice is forced. And I argue that this is even more true today, when 'authoritarian democracy' or 'populism' present themselves as alternatives to neoliberalism, while they are in fact functional to the 'perfect crisis' of the spontaneous order of the market.

---

48   Hayek, *Law, Legislation and Liberty*, p. 484.

III. FORMS OF LIFE

It is when the disease is at its height that it is necessary to use the most restricted regimen.

Hippocrates, 'Aphorisms', I, 8

9
Precariat

As with any medical crisis, the diagnosis of a disease always involves binding instructions on the conduct to follow in order to survive, heal, and recover from the disease. As Hippocrates reminds us, the more severe and advanced the disease is, the more stringent and restrictive the instructions that those who are subject to it will have to follow. Thus, a severe disease would require an *austerity* regime. The biopolitical crisis involves, therefore, a powerful process of subjectification as its intrinsic element, which configures our existence in a constant state of suspension between life and death. This condition becomes the rule in the spontaneous order of the market; it is in fact as a *dispositif* of an order – and not as a 'technical' and temporary factor of imbalance in the equilibrium of economic cycles – that the crisis involves and activates those subjective states of mind such as trust, credit, belief, guilt, expectation, fear, and sacrifice, induced by this condition of a suspension between life and death.[1] And the crisis profits from them.

---

1   On the psychic and emotional dimension of the neoliberal debt crisis,

By defining the order of the market as *cosmos*, Hayek distinguishes it from an economic order in the technical sense: 'While an economy proper is an organization in the technical sense in which we have defined that term, that is, a deliberate arrangement of the use of the means which are known to some single agency, the cosmos of the market neither is nor could be governed by such a single scale of ends; it serves the multiplicity of separate and incommensurable ends of all its separate members.'[2] The moment the consideration of the end in the dynamics of the market is lost, the only criterion that Adam Smith's classic liberalism assigns to it is rejected: the well-being of the community as a spontaneous result – the theory of the 'invisible hand' – of the initiative of individuals oriented towards selfish interest. Without such a measurable value, the market no longer responds to economy in a strict sense, but configures itself as a cosmos.

Being inscribed in the cosmos of the market, being part of it, has another consequence that – as mentioned above – strongly affects the processes of subjectification produced by neoliberal rationality: the subjects involved in the cosmos have a limited ability to understand and grasp its overall design and, therefore, to master the fate of their own actions:

Its degree of complexity [of the spontaneous order or kosmos] is not limited to what a human mind can master. Its existence need not

---

see E. Stimilli, *Debt and Guilt*, London: Bloomsbury, 2019. On the 'sacrifice' in both religious and moral-political senses (invoked for example by the austerity policies in the Southern European countries), see W. Brown, *Undoing the Demos: Neoliberalism's Stealth Revolution*, New York: Zone Books, 2017; and, in more general terms, J. Butler, *The Psychic Life of Power: Theories in Subjection*, Stanford: Stanford University Press, 1997.

2   Hayek, *Law, Legislation and Liberty*, p. 108.

manifest itself to our senses but may be based on purely abstract relations which we can only mentally reconstruct. And not having been made it cannot legitimately be said to have a particular purpose, although our awareness of its existence may be extremely important for our successful pursuit of a great variety of different purposes.[3]

The rationality of the order of the cosmos – be it natural or divine – is superhuman. The neoliberal cosmos thus actualizes an ancient conception of the human condition: 'Man is not and never will be the master of his fate: his very reason always progresses by leading him into the unknown and unforeseen where he learns new things.'[4]

Foucault described the process of subjectification activated by living within the cosmic order of the market. For him, the peculiarity of liberal governmentality is the 'live dangerously' imperative – that is, to live exposed to the constant threat of death: 'First, we can say that the motto of liberalism is: "Live dangerously." "Live dangerously," that is to say, individuals are constantly exposed to danger, or rather, they are conditioned to experience their situation, their life, their present, and their future as containing danger. I think this kind of stimulus of danger will be one of the major implications of liberalism.'[5] However, it is important to note that neoliberal governmentality is the 'threat' of death, the configuration of an existential condition that prompts one to safeguard and preserve one's own life within the only order that seems to guarantee survival. With the aim of surviving in the cosmos, one's life becomes the

3 Ibid., p. 38.
4 Ibid., p. 507.
5 Foucault, *The Birth of Biopolitics*, p. 66.

subject of constant adaptation. This adaptation is configured in 'living dangerously', in entrepreneurial risk, an indispensable condition for gaining the trust of the market, in order to compete within it. The shaping of the subjects' own forms of life to adapt to the cosmic order of the market – and therefore not to obey the sovereign order – is an essential aspect of biopolitical governmentality. In this sense it corresponds to the definition of biopolitics Foucault provided in *The Will to Knowledge*: 'a power to foster life or disallow it to the point of death'.[6]

If the current crisis is configured at a biopolitical level, then it is at this level that the processes of subjectification and the conflict they activate in society should be considered: the precariat is the child of *this* crisis, which, in exchange for survival, seems to condemn it to this condition with no alternative. This condition binds survival to continuous 'adaptation' to the changing and mutable circumstances of the market. These circumstances expose the precariat's existence to a sort of 'fate' over which it has no control, and which configures the time of life in the natural and biological sense, as the cyclical repetition of an eternal present. This indifference of the order to the fate of individuals, however, does not justify a fatalistic acceptance of one's condition, but rather requires the strengthening of one's ability to adapt and the acceleration of the rhythms of life.[7]

---

6   M. Foucault, *The Will to Knowledge: The History of Sexuality, Volume 1*, New York: Pantheon Books, 1978 [1976], p. 138.

7   The debate on 'acceleration' also considers the figure of precariousness as a peculiar product of the temporality of late modernity. See H. Rosa, *Alienation and Acceleration: Towards a Critical Theory of Late-Modern Temporality*, Copenhagen: NSU Press, 2010. See also J. Crary, *24/7: Late Capitalism and the Ends of Sleep*, London: Verso, 2013.

Therefore, we allow our 'plasticity' – our capacity as forms of life to interact with the environment by actively and creatively reacting to its changes – to become adaptation, and thus 'flexibility'.[8] However, no single individual is able to adapt to keep up with the pace of the reproduction of their form of life in order to compete on the market.[9] The precariat is, above all, the condition of life determined by the position of the individual human being within the cosmos of the market.

As such, it is only the life of precarious workers that holds together the broken fragments of their working selves, which are often in opposition, and which push them into forced decisions, as if they were suspended between life and death. Thus, the choice only *seems* free. No external command or order obligates the precarious worker to make a given choice, but no choice can be free within the *dispositif* of biopolitical crisis: it is, rather, a choice between life and death, therefore it is forced.[10]

---

8 See C. Malabou, *What Should We Do with Our Brain?*, New York: Fordham University Press, 2008. Malabou stresses the difference between flexibility and plasticity also from a neuronal and biological point of view: plasticity entails a conflictual relationship with the environment which does not tend solely to adaptation.

9 On the paradigm of the political economy of 'reproduction' proposed by feminist thought, see S. Federici, *Caliban and the Witch: Women, the Body and Primitive Accumulation*, New York: Autonomedia, 2004.

10 That the freedom of choice advocated by neoliberalism is only ostensible can be inferred by taking into consideration not only the figure of the entrepreneur, but also that of the consumer. For Colin Crouch, indeed, the priority attributed to 'consumer well-being' to the detriment of the consumer's freedom of choice is one of the peculiar traits of the neoliberal market. For this reason, the market sees the dominance of 'giant companies', i.e. transnational companies which now operate in their sector as a monopoly and which have not only the economic but also the political and juridical power to colonize the needs and the imaginary of consumers, thus predetermining their 'well-being': 'While consumer choice is a democratic concept, leaving decisions to consumers themselves, consumer welfare is a technocratic one;

The oscillation and ambiguity of the precariat between conservation and innovation and between cooperation and competition is explored in Paolo Virno's analysis of the multitude.[11] As Virno argued *mutatis mutandis* with regard to the multitude, the conflictuality of precarious workers is eventually turned against them, in a sense of guilt and indebtedness,[12] and, in the form of competition, against those who share their condition. Therefore, every decision produces new contrapositions without solutions. This is the consequence of a conflictuality that cannot be reduced to the modern dualistic and binary formulas that characterized much of twentieth-century philosophy and politics (as in Carl Schmitt's friend-enemy opposition) and that also configured class struggle: the precariat does not have a definite class enemy. The precariat cannot be exhaustively defined as a socio-economic class. Precariousness is rather a *form of life*:[13] that form of life that results from the neoliberal government of human resources in pursuit of profit.[14]

The art of the government of the biopolitical crisis does not offer the alternatives that used to fuel class conflict in the modern political crisis. Yet, although it is only today that the neoliberal art of government has made the precariat's form of

---

judges and economists decide what is good for consumers.' C. Crouch, *The Strange Non-Death of Neoliberalism*, Cambridge: Polity, 2011, p. 55.

11   See P. Virno, *Multitude: Between Innovation and Negation*, Los Angeles: Semiotext(e), 2008.

12   See E. Stimilli, *The Debt of the Living: Ascesis and Capitalism*, Albany: SUNY Press, 2017 [2011]; M. Lazzarato, *The Making of the Indebted Man: An Essay on the Neoliberal Condition*, Los Angeles: Semiotext(e), 2012 [2011].

13   It is on the definition of the precariat in terms of class that I disagree with Guy Standing's analysis, important though it is, in his *The Precariat: The New Dangerous Class*, London: Bloomsbury, 2011.

14   See M. Nicoli, *Le risorse umane*, Rome: Ediesse, 2015.

life predominant, this is not the first time that such a form of life has emerged historically. In the past, its aspect was ambiguous, indefinite, and incomprehensible because it didn't follow the process of political subjectification dictated first by the struggle for citizenship and then by class conflict. But some thinkers have been able to identify and recognize its character, meaning that it is possible to outline its genealogy.

10
The Paris of the Second Empire: The Hero and the Cosmos

Walter Benjamin is an essential turning point in the genealogy of the form of life of the precariat. Benjamin used the life and work of Charles Baudelaire as a litmus test in the archaeology of nineteenth-century Paris. In the same period in which the term 'crisis' fully entered into the economic lexicon, Benjamin saw this form of life appear, get captured and put to work within a new phase of capitalism, a form of life that would later become capitalism's typical form of life.[1] It was the heterogeneous and varied mass called the *bohème* that in 1848 built barricades against the Restoration, together with the proletariat and the liberal bourgeoisie. In his analysis of the events that led to the coup of 1852 in *The Eighteenth Brumaire of Louis Bonaparte*, Marx expressed a very negative opinion of the *bohème*,

---

1 On the capitalistic employment of initiative and relative work autonomy, including the so-called 'artistic critique', see L. Boltanski and E. Chiapello, *The New Spirit of Capitalism*, London: Verso, 2007.

calling it the 'scum of all classes'.[2] He recognized a fundamental ambiguity in it that made it susceptible to the lure of power, because it did not have any sense of class belonging. The form of life of the precariat therefore has ancestors in a series of figures belonging to the *bohème* – the *flâneur*, the idle, the conspirator by profession, the player, the night owl, the detective, the rag vendor, the prostitute, the poet, the artist – that were outside the market when they appeared on the Parisian scene, because their production escaped exchange value and commodification. Here is how Benjamin captures a snapshot of the *bohème* just before it was absorbed into the labour market:

> In Baudelaire's Paris things had not come to pass ... Arcades where the *flâneur* would not be exposed to the sight of carriages that did not recognize pedestrians as rivals were enjoying undiminished popularity. There was the pedestrian who wedged himself into the crowd, but there was also the *flâneur* who demanded elbow room and was unwilling to forego the life of a gentleman of leisure. His leisurely appearance as a personality is his protest against the division of labor which makes people into specialists. It is also his

---

2 'Alongside decayed roués with dubious means of subsistence and of dubious origin, alongside ruined and adventurous offshoots of the bourgeoisie, were vagabonds, discharged soldiers, discharged jailbirds, escaped galley slaves, rogues, mountebanks, lazzaroni, pickpockets, tricksters, gamblers, maquereaus, brothel keepers, porters, literati, organgrinders, rag-pickers, knife grinders, tinkers, beggars – in short, the whole indefinite, disintegrated mass, thrown hither and thither, which the French term la bohème ... This Bonaparte, who constitutes himself chief of the lumpenproletariat, who here alone rediscovers in mass form the interests which he personally pursues, who recognises in this scum, offal, refuse of all classes the only class upon which he can base himself unconditionally, is the real Bonaparte, the Bonaparte sans phrase.' Marx, *The Eighteenth Brumaire of Louis Bonaparte*, p. 149. For a historical profile of *bohème*, see E. Traverso, *Bohemia, Exile and Revolution: Notes on Marx, Benjamin and Trotsky*, 'Historical Materialism', 10:1, 2002, pp. 123–53.

protest against their industriousness ... But this attitude did not
prevail; Taylor, who popularized the watchword 'Down with daw-
dling!' carried the day.[3]

And this is how, for Benjamin, the metamorphosis takes place
and this form of life – which is born out of the market – becomes
a commodity among others and is put to work:

> In these conditions ... the gesture of the *flânerie* becomes mean-
> ingless for the free intelligentsia and therefore loses all meaning.
> Now the type of the *flâneur* so to speak shrinks, as if a bad fairy
> had touched him with a magic wand. At the end of this process
> of shrinking is the sandwich-man: here the identification with the
> commodity is complete. The *flâneur* is now really a commodity. He
> now goes for a walk for money, and his inspection of the market has
> become, almost overnight, a job.[4]

According to Benjamin, the forms of life to be found in
nineteenth-century Paris had a double alternative to the
strong model of the state of Napoleon III's Second Empire:
the market and the Commune. Baudelaire chose the market,
which appeared to him as the alternative to the extinction of
his own form of life in the 'people's community' of the state:
'This "crowd," in which the flaneur takes delight, is just the
empty mold with which, seventy years later, the *Volksgemein-
schaft* (people's community) was cast.'[5] He chose to sacrifice his

3   W. Benjamin, *Charles Baudelaire: A Lyric Poet in the Era of High Capitalism*, London: Verso/NLB, 1973, pp. 53–4.

4   W. Benjamin, *Baudelairiana. Unveröffentlichte Fragmente zu einer
Neufassung des Flaneurs*, 'Frankfurter Adorno Blätter', IV, 1995, pp. 13–14
(translation by SP).

5   W. Benjamin, *The Arcades Project*, Cambridge, MA: The Belknap
Press, 1999, p. 345.

poet's halo – the aura that kept poetry 'out of the market' – in order to save his life, and survive in the anonymous crowd of the metropolis and in the traffic of the boulevards, which had been created in Haussmann's urban revolution in the decades following 1848.[6] According to Benjamin, the market seemed to Baudelaire a refuge in which he could preserve his form of life, and where he could stand out, while bourgeois citizenship proclaimed equality. However, to make this possible, this form of life had to 'shrink' and take the exact features of the 'individual' who lived it. In other words, Baudelaire had to become 'his own impresario', the model of the neoliberal individual that Foucault calls the 'entrepreneur of the self'. The 'loss of the poet's halo' meant that it was not his poetry that allowed him to stay in the market, but rather his very form of life, which became the commodity to be promoted. In short, Baudelaire attached 'exhibition value' to his own life, well before this became the prerogative of the regime of visibility and self-promotion on social media and elsewhere:

No study of Baudelaire can fully explore the vitality of its subject without dealing with the image of his life. This image was actually determined by the fact that he was the first to realize, and in the most productive way, that the bourgeoisie was about to annul its contract with the poet. Which social contract would replace it? That question could not be addressed to any class; only the market and its crises could provide an answer … But the medium of the market through which it revealed itself to him dictated a mode of production and of living which differed sharply from those known

---

6   On Haussmann's urban revolution and the corresponding transformation in capitalism, see D. Harvey, *Paris, Capital of Modernity*, Abingdon: Routledge, 2006.

to earlier poets. Baudelaire was obliged to lay claim to the dignity of the poet in a society that had no more dignity of any kind to confer ... In Baudelaire, the poet for the first time stakes a claim to exhibition value. Baudelaire was his own impresario. The *perte d'auréole* concerned the poet first of all.[7]

Baudelaire attributed those 'heroic' traits that would distinguish him from the crowd to this eccentricity, to this originality – the mask of the dandy, of the 'outsider', which he consciously wore and describes thus:

> Dandyism appears especially in those periods of transition when democracy has not yet become all-powerful, and when aristocracy is only partially weakened and discredited. In the confusion of such times, a certain number of men, disenchanted and leisured 'outsiders', but all of them richly endowed with native energy, may conceive the idea of establishing a new kind of aristocracy, all the more difficult to break down because established on the most precious, the most indestructible faculties, on the divine gifts that neither work nor money can give. Dandyism is the last flicker of heroism in decadent ages.[8]

In this period of transition, dandyism represents, for Baudelaire, 'a new kind of aristocracy'. Bourgeois democracy is not able to recognize its values, because it does not attribute importance to a heroic singularity that strives to stand out from the crowd, but instead relegates it to the margins of

---

7   W. Benjamin, 'Central Park', in *Selected Writings, Volume 4*, pp. 168–9.
8   C. Baudelaire, *The Painter of Modern Life*, London: Penguin, 2010, p. 68.

citizenship. The hero's form of life finds its homeland only in the market:

> Baudelaire guarded this threshold [which separated the individual from the crowd], and that differentiated him from Victor Hugo. But he resembled him too, since he, like Hugo, failed to see through the social semblance which is precipitated in the crowd. He therefore placed it in opposition to a model which was as uncritical as Hugo's conception of the crowd. This model was the hero. While Victor Hugo was celebrating the crowd as the hero of a modern epic, Baudelaire was seeking a refuge for the hero among the masses of the big city. Hugo placed himself in the crowd as a *citoyen*; Baudelaire divorced himself from the crowd as a hero.[9]

However, as in classical tragedy, the figure of the hero is part of a dimension which encompasses and subsumes them, although in a different way from the 'mediocrity' of citizenship. Indeed, there is a cosmic order also for the modern hero, to which they have to submit and finally succumb. In modernity – as Hayek argues – the market takes the place of the cosmic order. That indistinct uniformity in the mass of citizens of the metropolis from which Baudelaire escaped will eventually be found on another level and with another and far more demonic quality. It will be found in the market:

> Baudelaire certainly did not hold in high consideration the égalité that the great revolution had written on his flag. He was not fond of the ideals of the Enlightenment ... Baudelaire hated the

---

9   W. Benjamin, 'The Paris of the Second Empire in Baudelaire', in *Selected Writings, Volume 4*, p. 39.

bourgeoisie, but his was a frenzied passion that overtook him at
times and then left him. He never understood its economic order
... The mirage of equality, which appears on the horizon of the
universal market, was the homeland of his poetic genius.[10]

In order to be 'outside', to earn a space of excellence and
individuality and stand out from the mass of the metropolis,
Baudelaire *entered* the market, where everyone is an individual
and all individuals are equal – that is, are subject to the same
'fate'.

In 1848, Baudelaire and the *bohème* were alongside the proletariat on the barricades, the latter being led by Louis-Auguste
Blanqui, the most influential 'professional revolutionary' of the
entire nineteenth century. In 1872, jailed after the repression of
the Commune, Blanqui wrote *Eternity Through the Stars* from
his cell. It laid out a cosmological vision marked by necessity and repetition. For Benjamin, this was an extraordinary
anticipation of Nietzsche's theory of the eternal return and an
expression of the resignation of the defeated revolutionary. In
Blanqui's cosmos, there was no space for Baudelaire's heroism,
not even one inexorably destined to failure. Every human
enterprise was always already planned in its entirety within an
impassive and inscrutable order. And neither was it possible
to find in this cosmic order any progress or hierarchy of ends:

At the present hour the entire life of our planet, from its birth to its
death, unfolds, day by day, on myriads of twin-globes, with all its

---

10   W. Benjamin, *Neue Baudelairiana. Unveröffentliche Fragmente ʒu
einer Neufassung des* Flaneurs, in 'Frankfurter Adorno Blätter', IV, München:
edition text + kritik, 1995, pp. 14–15 (translation by SP).

crimes and misery. What we call progress is locked up on each earth and disappears with it. Always and everywhere, on the terrestrial camp, the same drama, the same set, on the same narrow stage, a noisy humanity infatuated by its own greatness, thinking itself to be the universe and inhabiting its prison like an immensity, only to drown soon along with the globe that has borne the burden of its pride with the deepest scorn. The same monotony, the same immobility in the foreign stars. The universe repeats itself endlessly and struts on its legs. Unfazed, eternity plays the same performance in the infinite.[11]

While they appear to be poles apart, Baudelaire's heroism and Blanqui's cosmological vision are both the result of the century of revolutions and of the capitalist market's trespassing of the borders of the state: on the one hand the poet entrepreneur of the self, who believes he can retain his alternative status within the market; on the other, an order impassive to the fate of humanity and its heroes, in which only its inscrutability and the absence of alternatives make failure tolerable. The cosmic order becomes the only and last resort for guaranteeing equality among human beings.

Today, with the twentieth century in between, Blanqui's cosmology might seem yet another oddity of the nineteenth century and of a Paris populated by eccentrics, but in fact his cosmos is fully included in the neoliberal discourse. It is now customary to define the peculiarities of neoliberalism both through the process of subjectification that turned the individual into an

---

11   L.-A. Blanqui, *Eternity by the Stars: An Astronomical Hypothetis* (1872), trans. Frank Chouraqui, New York-Berlin: Contra Mundum Press, 2013, p. 149.

'entrepreneur of the self' and through the concept of the market as a space capable of self-government (*governance*). And yet, as well as this general approach, on the basis of the genealogy I have outlined above, neoliberalism could also be defined as a particular articulation of the individual and of the cosmic order. In line with Baudelaire, we can now place the prototypes of the precariat traced by Benjamin in nineteenth-century Paris in Hayek's cosmic order of the market. The cosmos is thus a spontaneous order comprising only individuals with their specific ends; moreover, given that this order is inscrutable in itself, to think of a 'common' end would simply be irrational, because the only thing that individuals have in 'common' is their participation in a cosmos that has no end in itself, let alone a hierarchy of ends. Within the cosmic order, the individual identifies their form of life with the enterprise, and the success or failure of their enterprise is presented to them as a 'fate' that they cannot control:

> this adaptation to the general circumstances that surround him [the man who acts] is brought about by his observance of rules which he has not designed and often does not even know explicitly, although he is able to honour them in action. Or, to put this differently, our adaptation to our environment does not consist only, and perhaps not even chiefly, in an insight into the relations between cause and effect, but also in our actions being governed by rules adapted to the kind of world in which we live, that is, to circumstances which we are not aware of and which yet determine the pattern of our successful actions.[12]

---

12   Hayek, *Law, Legislation and Liberty*, pp. 12–13.

The cosmic order of the market does not depend on the success or failure of individual enterprises; indifference to individual destiny is a trait common both to the ancient conception of the cosmos and the cosmic order of the market. It is true that the idea of the cosmos is specific to Hayek and is not found in subsequent elaborations of the neoliberal model. However, the origin of such indifference and impassivity may well be traced back to the notion of cosmos: the algorithms that organize and order neoliberal capitalism do not correspond exactly to the mathematics of the Pythagorean model that characterized the ancient conception of the cosmos, but they still represent a mathematical *dispositif* that no single individual is able to master.[13] This – rather than equal opportunities for success – is the common condition of departure within the cosmos of the market. Yet, the cosmos's configuration according to any mathematical model produces in individuals a feeling that they can rely on, if not really trust in, the order,[14] which later leads them to take responsibility for the failure of their own enterprises.[15]

In the cosmic order of the market, technicians are called upon to govern the economic crisis of states. Similarly, 'technicians' are also entrusted with the cure of the psychological crisis that derives from individual failure. Psychotherapists Miguel Benasayag and Gérard Schmit consider themselves 'technicians of the crisis' in the neoliberal era of 'sad passions', and ask themselves:

---

13   That the neoliberal 'governance by numbers' is only the most recent manifestation of the promise of an 'impersonal government' is A. Supiot's claim in *Governance by Numbers*.

14   Martijn Konings derives the normative and governmental aspects of Hayek's idea of the cosmos of the market from the 'idea of neutrality' connected to it. See Konings, *Capital and Time*.

15   See A. Appadurai and N. Alexander, *Failure*, Cambridge: Polity, 2020.

'Is there an effective incapacity today to take on even a wide and generalized situation of anguish without considering it to be primarily a matter of technique?'[16] According to the authors of *Les passions tristes*, the psychological emergencies which, as technicians, they are called to intervene in are in fact 'crises in the crisis', individual distresses within the neoliberal crisis as a governmental art. The technicians of the psychological crisis cannot help people to overcome the distress. They can only attempt 'to stabilize them in the crisis', and can only 'respond to emergencies, because crisis has become their permanent condition'.[17]

---

16   M. Benasayag and G. Schmit, *Les passions tristes. Souffrance psychique et crise sociale*, Paris: La Découverte, 2006 [2003], p. 8 (translation by SP).

17   Ibid., p. 14.

11
For a New Cosmos:
Decision without Judgment

On the basis of the genealogy here outlined, we could summarize the fundamental difference between neoliberalism – at least in Hayek's understanding of it, which sets its 'political vision'[1] – and classical liberalism as follows: while the latter presupposes individuals, and the market as the proper space for their actions, interrelationship and sociality, neoliberalism presupposes a cosmic order that produces its own peculiar form of individuality. Our era's prehistory is nineteenth-century Paris, when the figure of the entrepreneur of the self and its fate began to take shape.

---

1 Wolfgang Streeck defines the entire neoliberal project as 'Hayekian liberalization' – whose hegemony (and crisis) starts from the 1970s – and emphasizes some of its characteristics which are relevant for us: '*policy decisions* can be attributed to particular individuals or institutions, which can therefore be held accountable for them, whereas *market judgments* – especially if the market is assumed to be a state of nature – seem to fall from the sky without human intervention and have to be accepted as a fate behind which lurks a higher meaning intelligible only to experts'. W. Streeck, *Buying Time: The Delayed Crisis of Democratic Capitalism*, London: Verso, 2014, p. 62.

Up until the 1970s, Benjamin's outsiders participated only marginally in the great class conflicts and crises of the twentieth century. This form of life re-emerged with all its peculiarities with the onset of the post-Fordist mode of production in the '70s. It was also then that the neoliberal crisis began, today appearing as a biopolitical crisis that gives this form of life its peculiar traits. But if, in Baudelaire's time, the market seemed to be an alternative to extinction and death, for the *flâneur* today, the biopolitical crisis does not pose any alternatives. Moreover, since class conflict is no longer capable of posing alternatives outside of the neoliberal market, the notion of conflict turns into a function of government.

Defining the 'neo-capitalism' that was beginning to colonize Italian society in the early 1970s, Pier Paolo Pasolini said: 'All of the difficulty of judgment derives from the fact that we are entering in a moment of variants (of variations).'[2] In the neo-capitalism prophesied by Pasolini as a continuous proposition of variants and variations, judgment is 'without decision'. As we have seen, in the modern era judgment would trigger a conflict between alternatives, which would end with a solution. But today, without a political decision produced by the conflict, what appears as a choice between alternatives is in fact a variation that remains within the judgment and so does not resolve the crisis. As a matter of fact, the terms posed by the judgment constitute not an alternative but an alternation (for there is an alternative only if there is a political decision). In short, without a decision, this alternation leaves no alternatives. The most

---

2   P.P. Pasolini, 'The Dream of the Centaur: Reflections on the Sacred and the Bourgeoisie', in R. West-A. Maggi (ed.), *Scrittori inconvenienti: Essays on and by Pier Paolo Pasolini and Gianni Celati*, Ravenna: Longo, 2009, p. 144.

emblematic representation of this 'judgment without decision' is the degradation of the for-and-against practice of Enlightenment criticism – which is at the origin of modern conflict – to the 'Like/Dislike' of social media, undermining Kant's effort in the *Critique of Judgment* not to reduce judgment to individual feelings of pleasure and displeasure. It is precisely through the judgment of the 'Like/Dislike' that the socialization of the neoliberal individual occurs. The neoliberal mode of criticism must be 'immanent', consistent and compatible with the norms of conduct functional to the preservation of order: this means the loss of criticism's subversive scope of renewal, since it does not result in a decisive and final decision – the decisive crisis.[3] On the contrary, the individuals' precarious condition created by the neoliberal crisis fosters a widespread demand for security, which today dictates the political agendas of most Western and non-Western countries, and which often appears in the rhetoric that accompanies policies concerning migration. And so the precariat's conflictuality becomes politicised in this conservative way. Security, stability and order have become the watchwords of the biopolitics of the neoliberal crisis.[4]

It is necessary to conceive a practice of conflict that acts beyond the *dispositif* of subjectification and socialization already implemented by neoliberalism. In the current biopolitical context, conflict should not simply be conceived as a *dispositif*

---

3   'We shall call "immanent criticism" this sort of criticism that moves within a given system of rules and judges particular rules in terms of their consistency or compatibility with all other recognized rules in inducing the formation of a certain kind of order of actions.' Hayek, *Law, Legislation and Liberty*, p. 190.

4   See I. Lorey, *State of Insecurity: Government of the Precarious*, London: Verso, 2015 [2012].

of *division* and *competition*, which exposes life to the constant threat of death, and which demands adaptation to the context. If, in order to survive, forms of life must oppose one other, it is by relying on what they have in common that they might co-exist, in a conflict where the purpose of the one is not to outlive the other.[5] How, then, could we envision a conflict that shapes life without subjugating it, and that, instead of juxtaposing one form of life against the other, reveals and enhances *their being in common*?[6] If class politics broke with the people, today the *dispositifs* of neoliberalism – primarily the *dispositif* of crisis – neutralize this kind of conflict. In some ways, to insist on the dichotomous dimension, on a binary, would be functional to the neutralization already at work. It is time to rediscover the relational matrix of conflict, which runs parallel to the antago-nist matrix and works beyond and across classes. If thought of and practised *in common*, conflict could prove itself not only to be something that divides society, but also something that *makes* society. Conflict could therefore be the political practice of *how* we decide to co-exist, which expresses a being in common that is not defined by a common subjection within the same cosmos and the same fate. This is, in short, a conception of conflict that corresponds to an affirmative biopolitics: not a biopolitics that

---

5   I am suggesting, in other words, that we should conceive the *con-flict* on the basis of the meaning of the term *fligo*. The Latin verb *fligere* derives from the Greek and means 'compress, squeeze, crush, press'. Such 'being squeezed, pressed, crushed, compressed' could indicate not only the pressure exerted by the economic system on the life of precarious workers, but also a common life condition.

6   For a reconstruction of the debate in recent decades on the ontological conception of community, see G. Bird, *Containing Community: From Political Economy to Ontology in Agamben, Esposito, and Nancy*, Albany: SUNY Press, 2016.

imposes forced choices to guarantee the survival of the individual, but a biopolitics of potentiality, in which conflict is the
practice of deciding in common.[7] This is the condition that
would allow the precariat to institute its own politics as an alternative to the neoliberal market economy. Within an order of
survival that brings about precariousness, such a politics of life –
unlike a 'party of life' – does not impose a conflict *between* the
forms of life. In such a politics, conflict produces relations that
start a decision-making process: a politics *of* the forms of life.

To establish a politics of life, an alternative narration of the
cosmos should be produced to the one that makes forms of life
precarious, turning them into a 'human resource' to invest in
in order to survive. This would mean sharing another cosmos –
another order that promotes the potentiality of the forms of
life[8] – alternative to the cosmos of the neoliberal market, which,
in exchange for the recognition of the individual's place within
it, limits and reduces such potentiality to a 'capacity for adaptation'. Benjamin reminds us of that essential aspect of the ancient
experience of the cosmos that expresses the potentiality of the
human being as 'rapture' and which today we seem to have
forgotten.[9] The cosmos can be experienced as rapture only in
common, as an alternative to the individual's adaptation induced

---

7   The need for a 'decision-making' deriving from the 'assembly' of
the multitude is a fundamental theme in M. Hardt and A. Negri, *Assembly*, Oxford: Oxford University Press, 2017. For another recent theory of
assembly, which moves from the condition of precariousness, see J. Butler,
Notes Toward a Performative Theory of Assembly, Cambridge, MA: Harvard
University Press, 2015.

8   See R. Ciccarelli, *Forza lavoro. Il lato oscuro della rivoluzione digitale*,
Rome: DeriveApprodi, 2018.

9   I am grateful to Mauro Ponzi for the suggestion of translating the
German 'Rausch' as 'rapture'. See M. Ponzi, *Nietzsche's Nihilism in Walter
Benjamin*, London: Palgrave Macmillan, 2016.

by the neoliberal cosmos: 'The ancients' intercourse with the cosmos had been different: rapture (*Rausche*) ... This means, however, that man can be in ecstatic contact with the cosmos only communally. It is the dangerous error of modern men to regard this experience as unimportant and avoidable, and to consign it to the individual as the poetic infatuation of starry nights.'[10] Not only does this idea of the cosmos evoked by Benjamin recall some traits of Nietzsche's reflection on the Greeks, it also appears as an alternative to the idea of cosmos that the neoliberal market has turned into a governmental *dispositif*.

In the narrative of the neoliberal market cosmos, enjoyment belongs to the individual (we need only think of the critical literature on neoliberal hedonism typical of the 1990s),[11] and the failure to attain pleasure determines frustration, hence the prevalence of sad passions in our emotional states. In contrast, the rapture of the communal experience in the cosmos is the joyful elation that derives from a shared political form of life.

---

10   W. Benjamin, 'One-Way Street' [1928], in *Selected Writings, Volume 1*, p. 486 (translation modified).

11   Benjamin, however, saw already in Baudelaire's form of life the link between the exploitation of intellectual labour and individual enjoyment: 'insofar as a person, as labour power, is a commodity, there is no need for him to identify himself as such. The more conscious he becomes of his mode of existence, the mode imposed on him by the system of production, the more he proletarianizes himself, the more he will be gripped by the chilly breath of the commodity economy, and the less he will feel like empathizing with commodities. But things had not yet reached that point with the class of petty bourgeoisie to which Baudelaire belonged. On the scale we are dealing with here, this class was only at the beginning of its decline. Inevitably, many of its members would one day become aware of the commodity nature of their labour power. But this day had not yet come; until then, they were permitted (if one may put it this way) to pass the time. The very fact that their share could, at best, be enjoyment, but never power, made the period which history gave them a space for passing time.' W. Benjamin, 'The Paris of the Second Empire in Baudelaire', pp. 33–4.

The rapture of participation in a common form of life activates happy passions that the individual can enjoy.

The common link between the cosmos and the individual – which Benjamin so clearly calls into question – is not implicit in every conception of the cosmos but appeared in a specific historical and political conjuncture. The correspondence between the political order of the polis and the cosmic order failed with the Hellenistic period[12] – that is, with the decline of the political form of the polis and with the affirmation of the imperial form, the Macedonian first and the Roman later, a sort of globalization *ante litteram*. The rational order of the cosmos then became a refuge for the individual of Hellenistic philosophies, for whom the reference to a rational order no longer entailed being part of a political community, but, on the contrary, involved an escape from political life, which neither required nor foresaw the individual's participation.

In his genealogy of the 'care of the self', Foucault locates the transition from the Platonic exercise of this care – aimed at participation in political life – to the Hellenistic one, which saw the progressive separation of the individual care of the self from the political sphere: 'to be concerned with self in the Hellenistic and Roman periods is not exclusively a preparation for political life. Care of the self has become a universal principle. One must leave politics to take better care of the self.'[13] Thus, the imposition of a 'medical model' resulted in the individualization of the care of the self and the habit of a continuous practice, which

---

12   See L. Siedentop, *Inventing the Individual: The Origins of Western Liberalism*, London: Allen Lane, 2014.

13   M. Foucault, 'Technologies of the Self', in L.H. Martin, H. Gutman, and P.H. Hutton (eds.), *Technologies of the Self: A Seminar with Michel Foucault*, Amherst: Massachusetts University Press, 1988, pp. 30–1.

ended up coinciding with the entire existence of the individual: 'A medical model was substituted for Plato's pedagogical
model. The care of the self isn't another kind of pedagogy; it
has to become permanent medical care, which is one of the
central features of the care of the self. One must become the
doctor of oneself.'[14] In Hellenistic philosophies, the 'permanent
medical care' the individual has to receive corresponds to a separation between ethics and politics: moral conduct now defines
life, which is understood as individual life. Thus, the cosmos
represents an order that is beyond politics, although politics
guarantees the individual's universal citizenship. And so the
citizen of the polis becomes a citizen of the cosmos, a cosmopo-
lite. Having lost every direct or analogical link with the political
order, the Hellenistic cosmic order – the refuge and protection
of ethical and scientific rationality – set the conditions for the
autonomy of the individual and for the constitution of their own
private space. It was only in the modern age that this cosmic
order was broken, when the modern practice of criticism finally
bridged the gap between the individual and politics.

Similar to what happened with the decline of the ancient
polis, the decline of modern politics triggered a new globalization, which made room for new individualities demanding
an order different from that which modern politics was able
to guarantee and legitimize. To distinguish the current globalization from that inaugurated by Hellenism, Peter Sloterdijk
defines it as the 'Second Ecumene', emphasizing the peculiarity
of the individual forms of life that this cosmos determines:

---

14   Ibid., p. 31.

If the exemplary human in the First Ecumene was the wise man, who meditated on his dysfunctional relationship with the absolute, and the saint, who could feel closer to God than ordinary sinners through grace, then the exemplary human in the Second Ecumene is the celebrity, who will never understand why they had more success than other people, and the anonymous thinker, who opens themselves up to the two key experiences of the age: firstly, to the constantly recommencing 'revolutions' as the 'presentations of the infinite in the here and now', and secondly, to the shame which affects every thinking life today more than original sin: never rebelling enough against the ubiquitous degradation of all that lives.[15]

The forms of life of the neoliberal cosmos are marked by impotence: like the entrepreneur's success, the celebrity's success does not depend on personal merit and is not a sign of excellence, but is the favour accorded by fate to the individual's ability to adapt. The entrepreneur and the celebrity are both figures of the same form of individuality, which corresponds to that cosmos now colonized by the neoliberal market, whose quintessence is precariousness; that is to say, 'on markets, no one can be "at home"',[16] nobody can be master of their own destiny. Once again, this cosmos is entrusted with the rationality of the order and the criterion of just conduct. However, this time political life is not sacrificed; what is sacrificed is rather the autonomy and self-determination of the individual made possible by the Hellenistic cosmos and developed during the modern era and in liberalism. As we have seen, the cosmos

---

15   P. Sloterdijk, *Globes. Spheres, Volume II: Macrospherology*, Los Angeles: Semiotext(e), 2014 [1999], p. 948.

16   Ibid., p. 950.

of the neoliberal market involves an art of government. This is undoubtedly an essential difference from the Hellenistic cosmos, which configured its individualities sheltered from subjection to the imperial politics of the time, and yet the neoliberal market also remains essentially an articulation of the relationship between the cosmos and the individual. It is therefore necessary to think and act in another cosmos: not a cosmos for the life of the individual, but a cosmos of political life in common. Indeed, the *political* decision must come from life in common, from the common condition within a cosmos, as in Plato's *polis*. The *dispositif* of the neoliberal crisis neutralizes this decision, transforming the precariousness of individuals into the common condition in the cosmos.

We must therefore return to the 'rapture' that, for Benjamin reading Nietzsche, was the sign of an experience of the cosmos in common. In *The Birth of Tragedy*, Nietzsche characterizes the Apollonian in the Greek world as a 'trust' in the *principium individuationis* that dominates and orders the life of human beings through the 'beautiful semblance' that it gives to the individual: 'one could say that Apollo is the most sublime expression of imperturbable trust in this principle and of the calm sitting-there of the person trapped within it; one might even describe Apollo as the magnificent divine image of the *principium individuationis*, whose gestures and gaze speak to us of all the intense pleasure, wisdom and beauty of "semblance"'.[17] The original sense of human beings' belonging to the community manifests itself in the Dionysian rapture, from

17   F. Nietzsche, *The Birth of Tragedy*, in *The Birth of Tragedy and Other Writings*, ed. R. Guess and R. Speirs, Cambridge: Cambridge University Press, 1999, p. 17.

which the individual derives his potentiality: 'Singing and dancing, man expresses his sense of belonging to a higher community ... Man is no longer an artist, he has become a work of art: all nature's artistic power reveals itself here, amidst shivers of rapture (*Rausches*), to the highest, most blissful satisfaction of the primordial unity.'[18] Outside of this living in common, the power of the individual becomes the capacity for adaptation.

Deleuze also inherits the Nietzschean concept of Dionysian rapture. While Benjamin emphasizes the cosmos in common that it presupposes, Deleuze highlights another trait which is pivotal for my argument, that is, its irreducibility to the dimension of judgment: 'Whenever we turn away from judgment toward justice we enter into a dreamless sleep ... This dreamless sleep in which one nonetheless does not fall asleep, this insomnia that nonetheless sweeps the dream along as far as the insomnia extends – such is the state of Dionysian rapture, its way of escaping judgment.'[19] Although with different emphases, Deleuze and Benjamin both push their interpretations of Nietzschean rapture in the same direction: judgment is the essential tool of the cosmic order founded on the *principium individuationis*. This *dispositif* of individualization operates as the organization of bodies, more precisely as the organization of bodies reduced to 'organisms', as the mere function of an order:

18   Ibid., p. 26 (translation modified).
19   G. Deleuze, 'To Have Done with Judgment' [1993], in *Essays Critical and Clinical*, London: Verso, 1998, p. 130 (translation modified). Deleuze's text takes its cue from the 1947 radio programme by Antonin Artaud, *Pour en finir avec le jugement de dieu*.

judgment implies a veritable organization of the bodies through which it acts: organs are both judges and judged, and the judgment of God is nothing other than the power to organize to infinity … The body of the physical system is completely different; it escapes judgment all the more inasmuch as it is not an 'organism' and is deprived of this organization of the organs through which one judges and is judged.[20]

In struggle and conflict, Deleuze's 'body without organs' expresses its own power that doesn't adapt to judgment. This conflict is not 'against', but 'between' parts that through conflict do not oppose each other, but express their power in common. The conflict *between* parts is the conflict *of* the parts:

combat, combat everywhere; it is combat that replaces judgment. And, no doubt, the combat appears as a combat *against* judgment, against its authorities and its personae. But, more profoundly, it is the combatant himself who is the combat: the combat is *between* his own parts, between the forces that either subjugate or are sub-jugated, and between the powers that express these relations of force.[21]

This internal and external conflict of the precarious forms of life could be immensely powerful if its force were turned from competition and individual adaptation into sharing and common action. In fact, this is the only way to produce a decision autonomous from judgment, that is, a decision not predetermined by the crisis or functional to the organization of

20   Ibid., p. 130–1.
21   Ibid., p. 132.

the neoliberal cosmic order: 'A decision is not a judgment, nor is it the organic consequence of a judgment: it springs vitally from a whirlwind of forces that leads us into combat. It resolves the combat without suppressing or ending it.'[22]

Decision without judgment – not predetermined by judgment – might not seem very 'judicious', prudent or wise, if the political question par excellence remains 'what to do'. But decision without judgment consists in favouring the *how* over the *what* to do. Therefore, only the practice of a decision without judgment – a practice that consists in deciding in common a political form of life – could open up those alternatives that today the crisis forecloses. They don't appear in terms of a choice based on pros or cons, for or against, but they are certainly alternatives; alternatives that are real only if they are emancipated from the *dispositif* of crisis.

---

22   Ibid., p. 134.

Index